Showing Sheep

For Pleasure or Profit

By

Sue Kendrick

ISBN 978 1 90487 119 4
A catalogue record for this book is available from the
British Library

The Good Life Press Ltd.,
PO Box 536, Preston, PR2 9ZY

www.goodlifepress.co.uk
www.homefarmer.co.uk

Set by The Good Life Press Ltd.
Printed and bound in Great Britain by Cromwell Press

Showing Sheep

For Pleasure or Profit

By

Sue Kendrick

Contents

Foreword

One way or another, sheep have always had a part to play in my life. As a child growing up on my grandfather's farm, dipping, rolling fleeces at shearing and bottle feeding orphan lambs were all part of the yearly round that formed part and parcel of my childhood.

Later, married and embroiled in a long term cottage restoration project, I resurrected my farming interests by purchasing a couple of English goats and several "cade" lambs which we reared on the surplus goat milk and then dined very well on at the end of the summer.

During the eighties when my sheep enterprise began, you could buy cades through the markets

Showing Sheep

most weeks during the spring. A small lamb would cost you £3 and a strong one anything up to £15. This outlet provided a useful income for farmers with big flocks and little time to rear orphans or the spares from triplets or quads. Animal welfare regulations have now put paid to this practice and the only reason I mention it now is to illustrate the fact that it was, at that time, possible to turn a profit from sheep and even more so from pedigree animals.

Not that I was likely to get involved in pedigree breeding! Our quarter acre plot was just enough to support our goats and cades and with the growing demands of a young family to meet, the thought of setting up a "proper" sheep enterprise just never entered my head. That changed during the summer of 1989 when we were given the opportunity to rent 20 acres of land from the National Coal Board. As this ground was just yards from our cottage we didn't hesitate.

There were no buildings and only the ring fence was stock proof. As we were already keeping sheep, albeit lambs destined for our freezer, we decided a small flock of commercial sheep would be our best option. At the back of my mind I had some vague idea about finishing the resulting lambs and selling the meat at the farm gate. I had a friend at the time whose brother was a butcher and was already using him to slaughter and prepare our cades.

With this end in mind, we purchased twelve Cluns, beautiful sheep that I'd fallen in love with at the Royal Show and half a dozen Cheviot crosses. These came from a dealer and were all good strong ewes that had lambed twice before. By the way, if you are just starting with sheep, I wouldn't recommend you buy your first ewes this way! We were lucky, these sheep subsequently lambed well and prolifically, but without a little knowledge on our part, they could have proved a minefield.

This little flock was to be the basis of a small commercial enterprise consisting of rearing and finishing lambs on the grass which we had in abundance. Fate, however, chose to step in at this point. A visit to a country fair at Stoneleigh Abbey brought us into contact with Mr Michael Attwell. He had been exhibiting at the show and had a fine pen of six, in-lamb Suffolk, breeding ewes which he was using as a shop window to advertise the quality of his stock.

While I took two of my youngest children to answer the call of nature, my husband and father spent a delightful half hour being convinced of the benefits of pedigree breeding. Ever the business man, my husband quickly realised that by breeding terminal sires which is the chief purpose of the Suffolk, a bigger profit could be realised than by producing table lambs. By the time I returned from the inordinately long toilet queue, we were the proud owners of six pedigree Suffolk ewes all due to lamb the following January.

For a short while we ran this small pedigree flock alongside the Cluns and Cheviot crosses, but after

Showing Sheep

the first lambing season we sold the commercials and began to expand the Suffolks, eventually running a flock of over thirty ewes. The best of the ewe lambs were used as flock replacements and the best ram lambs sold as terminal sires at the autumn ram fairs. Inferior stock went to slaughter.

We were advised quite early in our sheep keeping career that showing and hopefully gaining a few prizes would help rack up prices in the sale ring, so in our second year as pedigree breeders we took the plunge.

Having shown a variety of animals over the years, we were not totally new to the showing experience. It was the preparation and clipping that proved the biggest challenge. Not being full time farmers and with a young family and a business to run, finding the time to practice and perfect the technique wasn't easy, especially when there were a host of other jobs that we had to contend with. For this reason we quickly confined our showing activities to a few easily reached shows within our locality.

These tended to be small affairs which usually ensured we had some success for we quickly found that we had chosen a highly competitive breed. Suffolks were being bred by a lot of farmers back then. It was the most popular of all the terminal sire breeds and the top flocks received big money for their best lambs. Unless newcomers had plenty of money to spend on foundation stock (which we didn't!) it wasn't easy competing against the big guns.

Nonetheless, the few years we spent travelling the smaller show circuit proved enjoyable and provided some great family days out. They also gave us the opportunity of meeting our prospective customers who often remembered us when it came to the autumn sales which of course, is one of the major reasons for showing.

With our engineering business expanding and off-spring beginning to pursue their own interests (no more cheap labour!) we began to find it more and more difficult to run the flock. Not wishing to give up sheep altogether we made the decision to cut the numbers to just twelve of our best ewes. This proved much more manageable and we concentrated on producing just a few ram and ewe lambs for the autumn sheep fairs. Don't, however, assume that even a flock of this size entails anything other than a lot of work

Finally I should like to say what a great pleasure writing this book has been and I should like to thank the many sheep breeders who took the time and trouble to help. Especially Mr. & Mrs. David Inman who made me very welcome at their farm and allowed me to photograph the process of clipping a ewe lamb from their Lindum flock destined for one of the first summer shows.

Chapter One
To Show - Or Not To Show

One thing really needs to be made clear from the outset; showing is hard work! Very hard work in fact! Not only do you have to spend time and effort in preparing your animals for the show ring, but you also have to be prepared to give up at least a day during the duration of the show and probably more than one if it is a really big show such as the Royal at Stoneleigh.

There will be a lot of hanging around between classes and you may have bad weather and other unpleasant conditions to contend with. Preparing for the show is also a time consuming process and begins well before the show date. Depending

Showing Sheep

on your chosen breed, you will need to acquire clipping skills and the necessary time to practice them. It's a big mistake to think you can pull a couple of ram lambs from the field the night before the show, give them a quick tidy up with the dagging shears and then expect to take a top prize the next day.

Mutal Support

On the plus side, the enthusiasm, friendliness and advice you will encounter from your fellow competitors is likely to be priceless. I've shown goats, cavies (which are guinea pigs), dogs and occasionally ponies. It doesn't matter what kind of animal you are presenting you'll always find that most people are more than willing to help a newcomer. Cynics might argue that this is only how it should be since the more people that compete, the greater the honour of winning. The truth is, most people that show animals have a real love of their stock and are very pleased to share their knowledge with newcomers who show signs of a similar appreciation.

When we first started with our Suffolks, we were very fortunate in having Mr Tom Harding who kept the Bentley flock living quite near to us. This was and still is one of the best flocks in the country which regularly figures in the top awards at many of the country shows around the area. In spite of his elevated status amongst Suffolk breeders, Tom very kindly invited me over to his farm and demonstrated how to clip and prepare a Suffolk ram lamb for show. Later in this book

To Show - Or Not To Show

I'll be explaining this in detail, but the practical advice you get from a hands on demonstration is worth far more than a tomb of text and pictures.

The Shepherd's Shop Window

Apart from the help and support you are likely to encounter from like minded enthusiasts, there is another very good reason why pedigree breeders show their animals. There has to be a market for the progeny you produce. Since there are heavy costs involved in rearing a pedigree animal, you need to do all you can to ensure as high a price as possible.

Showing is one way of bringing your stock to the notice of the buying public and can be thought of as the shepherd's shop window. Throughout the summer months country shows and fairs are staged throughout the country. Most of these will stage sheep classes and some will be used by breed societies to stage specialist classes of their own. The bigger shows will attract larger entries and the better quality flocks. Winning a coveted red rosette or indeed any coloured rosette at one of these shows is a real feather in a shepherd's cap and one that he or she will make the most of when it comes to selling stock at the autumn sheep fairs.

They are also great networking events. This has become something of a buzz word in the world of commerce in recent years, but farmers have been doing it for years around the shows and markets. Farmers in general are cautious folk and like to spend time looking at stock and discussing its

Showing Sheep

various merits with its owner before parting with hard earned cash. Making contact with prospective buyers and talking about your flock and farming practices during the social atmosphere of a show can do wonders when your stock comes under the hammer during the autumn sales.

Public Awareness

Something that many farmers have become increasingly aware of in recent years is the need to get the public on the side of British agriculture. Factory farming and intensive rearing systems have given farming a bad press in the eyes of the general public and the recent outbreaks of Foot and Mouth and Blue Tongue have done little to help. Being on hand to answer questions about their stock, its purpose and how it is reared can do much to restore confidence in an industry that seems to get hit by one catastrophe after another.

As breeders of Suffolk sheep, most of our lambs ended up as breeding stock and the rams as terminal sires to be crossed with Masham ewes for instance, producing commercial lambs for the British table. Other breeders who keep native breeds may be finishing their lambs for the end users and selling at the farm gate. Talking to the public at shows is a golden opportunity to create a customer base for their wares and in this ecologically aware age, explain the importance of buying locally to cut down food miles and gain health reassurances as to the wholesomeness of the produce.

To Show - Or Not To Show

The Various Types of Show

Shows come in all shapes and sizes, from the small country fete that may just have a couple of sheep classes covering all breeds, up to the large county shows including The Royal Show which takes place at Stoneleigh each July.

Each breed society will also run their own shows where entries will be restricted to its own breed. These shows are often run alongside a major agricultural society's own classes so the opportunity to gain more than one prize with a ram lamb say, is doubled as the potential is there to win a rosette in the Society show classes as well as the "open" classes put on by the agricultural show itself.

Agricultural shows and country fairs take place throughout the summer, usually on roughly the same dates each year. Show schedules will be made available quite early in the year and most shepherds will send for these as soon as they become available. There is a listing at the end of the book of the major shows staging sheep classes.

It makes sense to start with small events until you begin to get the hang of things, but if you are breeding animals that are destined to appeal to commercial sheep breeders such as Suffolks and Charolais then you really need to start competing at a higher level as soon as possible, otherwise you won't come to the notice of your potential customers.

Showing Sheep

The larger shows also tend to be better organised and more aware of a newcomer's problems as they will have dedicated stewards for the sheep sections rather than a hard pressed secretary who is taking entries and waving exhibitors in the general direction of a set of rickety outdoor pens.

Another important point to consider is that the top flocks and best judges will be at the larger shows so the opportunity of learning from these and measuring your stock against theirs is not to be dismissed lightly. For some breeders it will be fine to be a big fish in a small pool, but for others who are running their flock on commercial lines, a highly commended at a big county show is worth far more than red ribbons at the local church garden party.

Not For Me!

If by now you are thinking this showing business sounds like too much work and effort for rewards that could be a long time coming you would be quite justified in your thoughts, but there is no need to get rid of your pedigrees and start again with commercials.

You can still do well with pedigree sheep without joining the show circuit providing you have one of the breeds that are popular with commercial sheep breeders. By these I mean the Suffolk, Charolais or Blue De Maine. These sheep can be sold through mainstream markets, most of which will stage sheep and dedicated ram fairs throughout the autumn. Often these are held on special days apart from the normal market days and although sheep are not paraded individually in a ring, rosettes are awarded to those the auctioneer considers to be the best specimens.

Be warned though, to present your sheep at their best, especially ram lambs and shearlings which command the top prices, you will still have to prepare them as if for show by washing and clipping to accentuate their best features.

Obviously most of the animals presented will not be prize winners as the auctioneers offer limited awards. At the now defunct Market Bosworth cattle market a glass tankard was offered for the best ram lamb in the market. This went to one of our lambs along with a rosette and certainly helped to push up the price. Breeders will be putting forward possibly ten or even twenty animals at a time, so try and prepare well, at least in the case of your better animals in an effort to catch a potential bidder's eye.

Breeds of less interest to commercial breeders as terminal sires tend to remain clear of ordinary markets as prices generally tend to be very poor. The exception is the Rare Breed Shows and Sales which are put on by the Rare Breed Survival Trust. These sales are not just for sheep but also cover cattle and other animals. The show is often held one day and the sale the next. Not all stock is shown and some breeders who never show in the ring will put their stock forward in the sale ring and achieve realist prices provided the animal is well bred and nicely presented.

Some breed societies also have their own sales

Showing Sheep

and increasingly in this day and age almost every society has a web presence which often includes a discussion board or advertising section where photographs of stock can be posted for online perusal. As you can see various options are available if you really do not want to spend the summer at one agricultural show after another, but if you do and you begin to figure amongst the prizes, your stock will certainly be easier to sell.

For those that have now gone off the idea of showing, the following chapters on trimming and clipping will still prove worthwhile as it can only help when trying to catch a buyer's eye in the sale ring and the chapters on rearing and management are equally applicable to all sheep breeders so read on; you may find you take the plunge after all!

Chapter Two
Getting Started

If you haven't already started your flock then the best advice I can give is what was given to us when we first started – buy the very best you can afford! Translated into practical terms this means do some research on your chosen breed and find out which are the top flocks. Buying one or more of their lesser ewes is preferable to buying the best stock from an indifferent flock.

It's at this point I have to hold my hand up and say we did not initially do this. Our first six ewes came from a reasonably successful flock and formed a good basis, but with hindsight we were lucky. Buying on a whim is not a good way to start a

Showing Sheep

pedigree sheep breeding enterprise, especially in a highly competitive market like Suffolks which are one of the leading terminal sire producers.

Fortunately these ewes were in lamb to one of the breed's leading sires and our first lambs were of very good quality. The ewe lambs were added to the flock and the rams sold in the autumn ram sales as stock rams for commercial flocks.

Perhaps flushed with success, it was at this point we decided to sell the commercial flock of Cluns and Cheviot crosses and concentrate on breeding pedigree Suffolks. Our first aim was to build up numbers and introduce some other blood lines. Mindful of the advice we had been given, we went to most of the stock reduction and dispersal sales taking place during the next few months, buying just a few ewes or even just one at each sale.

This is quite feasible as unlike the commercial auctions you see in livestock markets, reduction and dispersal sales sell stock on an individual basis. A proper catalogue is produced which will give some history of the animal such as age, breeding, lambing history and often some information about her lambs if they have gone on to be show champions.

Going back to what was said at the beginning, buying a lesser ewe from a top flock proved a very good move for us. One of the dispersal sales we went to was the Wappenbury flock based in Worcestershire. This was owned by Mrs. M. R. T. Rimell who took it over on the death of her father, Sir William Lyons. This flock had been established for a very long time and had consistently produced champion sheep.

We bought a six year old ewe which was in-lamb to the flock's top stock ram. Normally you would not advise anyone to buy a ewe this old, but the fact that she was still in a flock of this calibre said a lot about her performance. In fact looking at her past history, several of her lambs had gone on to win prizes at high level competitions.

She produced a very fine pair of ram lambs which even a beginner could see were head and shoulders above anything we had previously bred. This ewe went on to produce another five crops of lambs, all of which were of excellent quality and sold well in the autumn sales. Her only fault, if it could be called a fault, was that she did not produce any ewe lambs. This was a bit unfortunate as she had been bought primarily to add the Wappenbury bloodline to our flock.

Inbreeding

Some people wouldn't have seen this as a problem as inbreeding is quite a common practice amongst some stockmen. It is argued that mating son to mother, father to daughter etc. is an excellent way to fix type and characteristics. This is probably so, but Suffolks are not easy sheep to lamb and the lambs themselves often lack vigour at birth in spite of their size. We felt a lot of these problems were caused by injudicious breeding so preferred to cross breed between the blood lines of different flocks.

Showing Sheep

During that summer and the following year we added ewes from the Santon flock owned by Mr. Sandy Fraser. We never used home bred rams but always went out to one of the top Suffolk breeders for a good ram lamb. This worked well for us as, apart from a short period of three or four years when our flock size reached around forty ewes, most of the time we kept numbers down to about twelve to fifteen.

Line Breeding

Another form of breeding we could have tried was line breeding. This is where you mate all your ewes to the best son of your stock ram. The next year you use his grandson and so on. Again we did not try this as, although we were buying the best rams we could afford, they were still not at the top end of the market.

Perhaps a little note about Suffolk breeding wouldn't be out of place here. When we started with this breed in the late eighties competition was very fierce. The main prizes at shows and sales were being fought over by a few top flocks and a rough hierarchy was in place. The best ram lambs and shearlings from these flocks would usually be sold to other flocks on the same level for what appeared to be huge sums running into thousands of pounds. In reality it was often only a few hundred pounds that actually changed hands as flock A would buy from flock B and vice-versa. Or perhaps flock A would buy from flock B and flock B from flock C and flock C from flock A. Flocks on a slightly lower level would also buy from the top flocks and then flocks below these would buy their stock and so on. In other words everyone was looking to buy from the next tier up.

This was quite understandable given that for many of these flock owners breeding top quality terminal sires and breeding stock formed a significant part of the farm income. Many of these flocks were badly hit during the 2001 foot and mouth epidemic with a lot either dispersing their flocks altogether, or making drastic reductions.

Keepers of rare and minority breeds will probably not see quite so much stiff competition, but even so, you should always buy from at least as good a flock as yours and preferably one that is better.

Buying Older Stock

As said earlier, buying older ewes is not something a newcomer to shepherding is generally advised to do, but pedigree sheep are a slightly different matter. They have been kept in the flock for a good reason and the reason is that they usually produce excellent lambs that go on to fetch good prices.

Once you have gained a little experience, you will soon see the truth of this as even with our system of frequently changing the ram, the same ewes consistently produced the best lambs and that is why we had ewes in our flock as old as twelve and thirteen. You will also notice that your flock naturally divides into specific families. Home bred replacements invariably are the ewe lambs originating from your best ewes.

When this pattern establishes itself it is a good idea to get rid of the poorer performing ewes as, to quote my father, "a bad 'un eats just as much as a good 'un!"

Expert Advice

Staying with good 'uns and bad 'uns for a moment longer, it's very tempting when your first crop of lambs arrive to view them through rose coloured spectacles and keep everything. The temptation to make allowances is even more likely if you only have a small flock and are desperate to start showing your own stock, but what you have to remember is that the judge will penalise breed faults and some really bad faults like an undershot or overshot jaw will get you disqualified.

If you can, try and get a breed expert to come and give your lambs the once over. This will save you a lot of heartache later on. Hopefully he will point out one or two potential show animals which should help you plan your feeding requirements. If you can't get someone to come and look at your stock, keep only the animals that conform really well to your breed specification and accept that some, possibly the majority, will have to go for slaughter.

Having said this, the situation is slightly different with Suffolks. Almost all stock is destined at least initially for the breeding market with the better stock going to the pedigree flocks and others as terminal sires for commercial flocks. Rams that don't get sold as lambs will either be run on for another year and sold as shearlings, or if the quality doesn't make it feasible, sent for slaughter. Of course it goes without saying any animal that has severe faults is destined for mint sauce from the outset.

Selecting Your Show Stock

You can in theory show stock that you have bought in as long as you are honest about who has bred the animal. As preparation and feeding play a big part in separating winners from losers you could be quite justified in taking credit for bringing on a lamb and showing it the following year as a shearling. I'm not sure people would take too kindly to you showing the current breed champion and sweeping the board at your local country fair though.

Most people prefer to show something that they have bred themselves and it is surprisingly quick how you can spot a potential show animal almost from the time of birth. Keeping in mind what the purpose of the animal is and being very familiar with the breed specification will be a great help.

A word of warning though! If your sheep are a hobby and a way of keeping grass down in a paddock, it is very easy to lose sight of what a sheep's purpose actually is, ie. to provide meat and wool. It isn't winning rosettes and cups in a summer show ring. It's important to keep this in mind as the last thing that breeders of any breed of sheep should do is breed for cosmetic appearances. A particular shaped head, for instance. I famously heard a couple of judges discussing the merits of a Suffolk ram where one remarked to the other that the animal had a "nice head."

"Heads is two a penny on a butchers slab!" the other remarked drily.

When selecting potential show stock there are always certain things to look out for. Good sized lambs without any obvious breed faults with long backs, deep chests and broad rear ends were the main requirements. Also keep a note of growth rate as one of the Suffolk's attributes is its ability to mature early which is much prized amongst commercial flock owners. Large flocks often record this at regular intervals and measure it against food intake, but our numbers were relatively small so we tended to rely on our eyes.

Culling

Before leaving this chapter it's worth mentioning that after your first year with your foundation flock you will almost certainly have encountered a few problems, not necessarily because you have been sold "a pup," but more likely because sheep are sensitive creatures and upsetting their routine can make them prone to various afflictions that they never encountered in their previous homes.

We've already mentioned sending sub-standard lambs to slaughter, but you should also cull troublesome or under performing ewes as well. We usually did this at weaning and sometimes early autumn if persistent problems arose during the summer. We had one ewe that developed chronic footrot. In spite of regular foot bathing, trimming and footrot vaccination, she regularly succumbed to bouts of infection which if not treated very quickly spread to other flock members. Although we culled her in the end, we had a couple of her daughters in the flock and they too were prone to rot and abscesses which leads me to think there is a hereditary factor involved.

After every lambing you'll also encounter, sooner or later, one or two ewes that have lost a "quarter." This is actually a misnomer as sheep don't have quarters. Their udder is separated into two halves so it should be lost a "half," but the cattle term losing a quarter due to mastitis or some other infection is generally used. A lot of shepherds will breed from these again the next year, especially if the flock is small. We did this for several years, but with hindsight it isn't something I'd advise. These ewes invariably had twins which meant the ewe seldom had enough milk to rear them both. You were faced with either supplementary feeding with a bottle or removing one altogether and either bottle feeding or attempting to get on another ewe. Whatever method you chose usually proved troublesome and ate into valuable time with the end result being at least one under performing lamb.

It's also far too easy to let these ewes build up so each year the problem is exacerbated. Much better to be ruthless and cull from the outset.

Chapter Three

Feeding

There's not a lot of difference between breeding pedigree sheep destined for the show ring or producing lambs for the table except that you will be feeding show stock for very much longer. Having said this, a lot of talk around the show ring centres around what goes down the champion's throat and secret recipes abound.

Seriously though, all stock needs to be adequately fed otherwise your sheep enterprise is likely to flounder before it even starts. It doesn't matter how good your stock is or how well you prepare it for the show or sale ring, if you haven't provided enough good nutrition the animal will not attain the correct size or develop the full potential of its body conformation. "A good big 'un will always beat a good little 'un," as my father was fond of saying.

Flushing

The whole process begins long before the potential show champion makes its first appearance in the world. In fact it starts way back in the late summer or early autumn when the flock ewes need to be flushed.

This is a process where ewes are given some quality feed to encourage ovulation and the shedding of multiple eggs leading to an increase in the possibility of twin births. The most common way of doing this and the one we practiced is to have ready some fresh pasture of new grass. The aftermath of haymaking is ideal, especially if a little fertilizer is applied. This worked out well for us as most years we did not get our hay until July or sometimes even August if the weather was really unkind such as in the memorable summer of 2007.

Allowing one of the meadows to grow on after the cut usually produces a nice "bite" by early August which is when we flushed the ewes and introduced the ram. If this seems a little on the early side, the reason is that pedigree lambs need to be born during January or February to allow enough time to make the necessary growth to be shown at the summer shows and sold during the autumn sales. In fact, some breed societies have relaxed their rules to allow lambing in December or November.

Showing Sheep

As with any move to clean pasture, it is always a good idea to worm the flock, check and trim feet and run through a footbath if used or check that your footrot vaccination programme is up to date.

Grass isn't the only way of flushing, so if you have a very small acreage, don't despair! You can simply feed a small portion of cake once a day. Half a kilo should be enough. Ewe nuts are convenient and should be around 16% - 18% but you can also use a home mix which we'll be looking at later in the chapter. Some shepherds, if they have very thin ewes, will offer cake even though they are grass flushing to get the optimum number of eggs a ewe needs to be in good condition, neither too fat nor too thin.

Other good feeds for flushing are root crops such as sugar beet and stubble turnips and various brassicas like kale which I have vivid memories of being grown on my grandfather's farm. As a small child I well remember getting completely lost amongst the tall, leafy plants. On larger holdings these are strip grazed with the aid of an electric fence that is moved once a day so that the crop is neatly and efficiently grazed without undue waste.

You can also get proprietary ewe flushers consisting of minerals and trace elements. These are fed for a few weeks before the ram is introduced and continued for few weeks afterwards. I can't personally vouch for these as we never used them, but we have used molasses mineral licks during tupping, lambing and rearing, so they probably amount to the same thing.

Grading

So how do you know whether a ewe is in the correct condition? With your own animals the answer is mainly by experience. When you've kept sheep for a while, you tend to develop a kind of sixth sense regarding the state of your flock and even though by August most ewes will have a good growth of wool on their backs, I can usually spot an animal that needs additional feeding simply by using my eyes. I suspect that this is greatly helped by the fact that most of our flock tended to err the other way and were too fat, which can happen when you keep small numbers and have plenty of good grazing.

That isn't very helpful for a novice, however, or for sheep that are not your own, so here's a rough and ready way of assessing condition. Put your hand on the backbone in the area around the thirteenth rib. You should only feel the bones when exerting a little pressure. If you feel them without pressure the ewe is too thin. If you have to press down hard or make a dent, then the ewe is too fat.

This is an adaptation of the standard grading process which is commonly used by shepherds and butchers to assess the condition of sheep. A scoring system is used ranging from 0 – 5. The optimum condition for a breeding ewe is between grade 3 and 4. This chart shows all the grades.

Showing Sheep

0	Hopefully you will never encounter this as the animal is nothing but skin and bone and is probably on the point of death.
1	The backbone is sharp and your fingers can pass under or between the vertebra.
2	The vertebrae are smooth and rounded with just a little elevation felt as corrugations. Can still feel around vertebra, but smooth.
3	The individual vertebra can just be felt, but are smooth. Ribs need firm pressure to be felt.
4	Backbone can only be felt by pressing lightly with the thumb. Individual ribs need firm pressure to be felt.
5	Backbone can only be felt by applying firm pressure. Ribs cannot be felt at all.

Steaming Up

Having got the ewes safely in lamb, the next stage in the journey leading to your world beating show champion is to ensure that its mother has adequate nutrition during the last few weeks of pregnancy to stave off the very real danger of twin lamb disease, a distressing condition that often results in dead lambs, blindness and a poor prognosis for the ewe.

The last six weeks of pregnancy places enormous demands on the ewe's body when she not only has to maintain herself, but must also provide for a rapidly growing lamb or lambs. To ensure that she maintains her own health and produces at least one fit, strong lamb or preferably two,

Feeding

you need to "steam up" by providing some high energy supplementary feed.

For January lambing you need to start the steaming up process mid-November by providing about a quarter of a kilogram of cake, gradually increasing to 1.5 kilograms by lambing. Remember, the bigger your sheep and the more prolific they are, the more cake they will need. Quantities here are based on Suffolk ewes which are large sheep and commonly the bearer of twins. Smaller sheep or hardy native types will not need these quantities.

Once you start feeding cake, the workload increases and there is a big temptation to offer the feed in one daily ration. This is a mistake as there seems to be an addictive quality to concentrate feeding that turns a healthy sheep into a greedy eater with the result that food tends to be bolted down. This can end in an alarming condition known as Acetosis which results in the ewe standing away from the trough, sneezing and coughing with heaving flanks, gaping mouth and a copious amount of white froth foaming around her mouth and nose.

She looks as if she is having a fit, but in fact she is just being sick. It can prove fatal so you need to keep an eye on the situation and if the blockage doesn't clear reasonably quickly call the vet. Although we have experienced this on several occasions with greedy lambs, it has never proved fatal as the patient recovered quickly, but it could be that we were just lucky. To cut down the risk of this happening, once concentrate feeding gets

Showing Sheep

to about half a kilogram per day, split it into two feeds and offer in the morning and evening.

One aspect of steaming up that is often overlooked is the need for adequate trough space. When it comes to getting their fair share of the tasty goodies arriving in those very recognisable buckets, sheep are sadly lacking in manners. A lot of shoving, butting and barging goes on and the shepherd is in real danger of being flattened in the rush.

There should be a minimum of 20 inches of trough space per ewe, although ewe lambs and small sheep may be able to get away with 15 inches. Don't forget though, if your sheep have horns they will need more. If you can set up a system whereby you can place food in the troughs from outside the pen you will find it much easier to feed with less risk of being knocked about. There are plenty of good handling and feeding systems on the market that should help with this or if you have the time and inclination you can construct your own from pallets or hurdles.

Whatever system you use, do make sure that troughs are clean and free from dung and bird droppings. This is very important as there are some diseases known to be spread by birds and even cats. Mindful of this, when feeding from troughs in fields or pens we always waited until the ewes had finished and then turned them over to prevent contamination.

In addition to cake, water and good quality hay or silage should also be available. We always fed hay ad-lib to all our animals, but some people do not like doing this as they think it is wasteful with a lot of good hay going to waste on the floor. Personally I think if you are feeding quality feed it will all get eaten sooner or later and it's much better for the sheep to have something to nibble on throughout the day which mimics natural behaviour rather than standing around getting bored.

The Growing Months

Lambs have the potential to grow very rapidly during the first few months of life so it is important to capitalise on this. As weaning approaches gradually reduce the amount of feed given to the ewes whilst increasing that offered to the lambs.

Obviously you have to devise some way of feeding lambs separately from the ewes which show no compunction about robbing their offspring of nourishment at every available opportunity.

During the early weeks we fed lamb creep feed. This is a small, high protein pellet that lambs quickly take to. A corner of the lambing shed should be cordoned off and creep feed placed in troughs or sometimes a commercially purchased combined hay and trough feeder depending on numbers. Always provide feed on an ad-lib basis, ie. available all the time and topped up as necessary.

The lambs also help themselves from the ewes' troughs as well, (providing they can worm their way in!) and this naturally gets them onto the bigger ewe nuts or other feeds that you may want to offer.

Showing Sheep

We tended to keep our lambs on an ad-lib system until at least weaning which generally takes place at around three months. Once this occurs split the crop into ewes and rams and run each group onto some good pasture of which there is usually an abundance as spring gets well underway. The feeding of concentrates should still continue as grass alone, no matter how good, will not achieve the growth rates needed for the summer shows or the autumn markets.

The one concession we made was to feed slightly less to our ewe lambs as we mostly only showed rams. As our flock was small, most of our ewe lambs were destined as flock replacements. Bigger flocks would probably grade their stock at this point and pull out potential show champions for specialised feeding, but as our numbers were too small to make this practical we had to content ourselves with dividing the sexes and sending any inferior specimens for slaughter as soon as they reached the optimum weight.

By weaning we liked to get our ram lambs onto about 1.25 – 1.5 kilograms (3lb – 3.5lb) and the ewe lambs on slightly less. A portable hay/trough feeder is very useful at this stage as it can easily be towed to different fields as stock is moved around. Continue to feed at these quantities throughout the summer and up to when the rams are sold at the autumn sales. If possible I should advise that they continue with some additional feeding during the following months, especially if being put to ewes, which most of ours were. As for the flock replacements, they should also continue to receive a small supplementary feed until about a year old.

At the Show

Although sheep are fairly adaptable creatures, shows are often quite stressful environments, especially for the first timer. This can make an animal prone to digestive upsets, the risk of which increases if new feeds are introduced. It makes sense to get your show stock used to a variety of feed during the growing period, especially cabbage which can be fed to prevent excessive thirst that could lead to bloat.

Some exhibitors offer this in preference to water during the run up to a class, but we never withheld water, preferring to keep the diet as close to that which was received at home as possible. This entailed taking our own hay and often a bag of grass which we scythed just before departure.

All the shows we attended provided hay and straw, but the bigger shows also provide grass. This is fine when it first arrives, but it quickly wilts and starts to ferment on a hot day so it's best to steer clear of it at this stage as it can have quite a dramatic effect on your stock who can stagger about as if drunk. To be on the safe side, it's better to take your scythe with you and cut your own.

You also need to take a little care with hay. A diet that consists of a high hay intake can push the front teeth out of line which may lead the judge to think the animal is overshot. This is an extremely bad conformation fault for any breed and will be heavily penalised. We never suffered with this as we were not frequent showers and between times our stock was turned out to grass. Other flock owners that follow the circuit weekend after weekend should keep an eye out as stock is often housed for long periods, especially if the weather is bad. Fortunately the problem usually corrects itself once grazing re-commences.

A slightly different problem arising from feeding hay relates to seeds and small stalks falling into eyes and fleeces. To prevent this we simply shook the hay out well and fed from the floor. Other shepherds use a sheet tied to the pen side from which the sheep reach inside to nibble. I've also seen hay nets used. Usually there is no problem with these, but you should be aware of the risk of getting limbs stuck or even a head if in poor repair.

Home Mixes

These are worth considering if you produce or have access to sugar beet or whole grains and, with the current rocketing in feed prices, are likely to become more popular, depending on what is available.

We were big fans of molassed sugar beet, especially during the middle to end of a ewe's lactating period when we would mix it with ewe nuts and oats or barley. Although sheep will eat it dry, we always soaked it over night so that it swelled. I would certainly suggest you did this if showing as feeding it dry can cause excessive thirst which you don't want to provoke just before entering the ring.

You can also buy fish meal or pellet mixes which often contain any of the following; soya, locust beans, flaked peas and various minerals and vitamins. These come out at 30% -50% protein which is too high for straight feeding, but by mixing with other feeds at about 10% can provide an excellent feed. Soya meal is another excellent source of protein, but again it needs to be mixed with grains, minerals and vitamins to provide a balanced ration. The chart below shows some examples of home mixes using soya meal. For steaming up pregnant ewes use at least 16% protein and preferably 17% - 18%.

Kg/tonne	Protein	Protein
	16%	18%
Barley	575	525
Molassed Sugar Beet Feed	200	200
Soya Bean Meal	175	225
Mineral	25	25
Molasses	25	25

Here's another very simple ration illustrated with small quantities which I find easier to get my head around, although far from being scientific.

A small handful of linseed cake for protein, mixed with six scoops of oats, wheat or barley, (preferred) and the same of sugar-beet, (the shreds and preferably molassed). By a scoop I mean the ones you can buy for ladling out horse food etc. It's a bit of a rough and ready mixture, but one we used for a while when we had access to some cheap

Showing Sheep

barley! The only problem with it was that some of the rams got a bit picky and wouldn't always clear up the barley. You also need to provide a mineral bucket or lick unless you add these to the mix.

It's a good mix for conditioning growing rams as judges like to see a tight, well muscled body rather than one that runs to fat. In fact we sometimes used to mix a little linseed oil into our commercial mixes as my father was convinced it gave the rams a little something "extra!"

Before leaving this chapter, a quick word of warning! Rams can develop kidney stones if fed magnesium. If feeding a home mix ensure that this is not included in any mineral element. Commercial mixes will state the ingredients on the bag so check or ask before purchasing. Similarly, if providing mineral buckets, select those specifically for male sheep.

Chapter Four

Housing

When I was growing up in the late fifties on my grandfather's farm, the only time sheep ever came inside was during shearing and for dipping. This had more to do with the convenience of a large covered crew yard than anything else. To suggest the flock "in wintered" would have caused the old boy to choke on his woodbines.

Grandpa, however, wasn't in the business of rearing pedigree sheep or showing them at the county shows so his flock lambed during March and April. For pedigree breeders looking to sell ram lambs as breeding stock at the autumn sheep fairs this is far too late as they are unlikely to achieve the necessary size by September/October.

Showing Sheep

In view of this most pedigree flocks aim to lamb during January and February which is often when we see the worst of the winter weather. For this reason many breeders elect to house their flocks, at least during lambing.

Housing is also necessary for winter shearing which is a requirement for many breeds that need to be trimmed for the summer shows.

We usually brought our Suffolks in at least two weeks before lambing and perhaps earlier, depending on the weather and the state of the fields. Some years it would be mid-December, others as early as November. We always felt it best to keep the flock out as long as possible, but much will depend on available acreage and weather conditions. Like most farming practices it tends to be a balancing act with gains on the swings being lost on the roundabouts. The withdrawal period when sheep are housed also helps to break the infield worm cycle which is a big bonus.

Personally speaking though, the biggest benefit of housing was lambing in the relative comfort of a large, airy shed. Even the most enthusiastic stock keeper can soon feel disheartened at what seems like endless nights of slopping around in mud, rain and howling gales trying to sort out the problems of a difficult birth.

As already mentioned, our housing is large and airy and was purpose built, replacing the ramshackle creations we first started with, but you don't need fancy state of the art buildings to house sheep. The idea is not to keep them warm, far from it!

Heat will cause them stress and can lead to all kinds of problems.

Almost any shelter will do as long as it offers protection from the worst of the elements and has a good air flow. Having said that, many of the old buildings to be seen around farms and smallholdings are often low roofed and windowless. They were not really designed to house animals full time, but served as milking parlours and stables. If you are going to use these for in-wintering sheep they need to be used with care as the air flow isn't usually that good and they are often difficult to clean properly after use.

The building we used has three sides enclosed by concrete panels with the fourth carrying feed barriers. This side is away from the prevailing wind and has an overhang to keep the barriers out of the wet. The building housed both our suckler herd and sheep flock, which happily existed side by side over the winter months.

Aware of the importance of air flow, we paid special attention to this during the design stage which is very important if you are to avoid respiratory problems. Sheep, like most animals, are prone to pneumonia if kept in badly ventilated buildings so you need to ensure that there is enough head room to allow the warm air to rise well above the flock with preferably some exit routes at eaves level.

Our building has its three enclosed sides finishing several feet short of the roof eaves. This allows a continuous through current of air and, during all the years since this barn was erected, we have never suffered a problem with pneumonia in either sheep or cattle.

This building was purchased from a specialist agricultural buildings manufacturer who was well aware of the needs of animal housing. These suppliers will have supplied buildings for all kinds of stock and management systems so it is worth listening to any advice they may give. The one we used, on hearing that we also intended to build a row of stables, came up with the suggestion of extending the roof and fitting these to the back of the barn. This saved us a considerable amount of space, not to mention money.

There are other options. Polytunnels with woven sides make excellent temporary housing and pole barns are versatile and fairly cheap options. We are big fans of pole barns since they are quick to erect and can be used to store hay and straw and, with the addition of rails and gates, can quickly be turned into cattle or sheep pens. They also double up as machinery stores when not in use for anything else.

Space

Although sheep are herd animals and are happiest when in a flock, they do need a reasonable amount of personal space otherwise fighting and bullying will break out. As most of the flock will at times be heavily pregnant, this is something that must be avoided as much as possible. How much space a ewe will need will vary somewhat according to breed and size, but around 10 to 15 square feet should suffice in most instances. You need to keep in mind that this will reduce considerably when lambs arrive so factor in some additional space to accommodate these.

You will also need to provide feed troughs. Individual buckets and bowls are fine for small numbers, but anything above 3 or 4 would be best served by troughs, as much for your own ease as anything. It's not much fun having half a dozen greedy ewes all trying to dive head first into your bucket. Troughs should give about 18 inches of space per sheep. We allowed about 2 feet for our Suffolks which are naturally big sheep anyway, but when heavily pregnant are positively huge.

Even so, there will still be some bullying and fighting. As with people, some ewes are naturally more dominant than others and you'll find that these will push and shove their way forward and claim all the best goodies. In fact, some can be so aggressive they will butt very timid ewes out of the way or even prevent them coming to the trough altogether.

Ensuring that there is adequate trough space can usually solve this problem, but if it persists you may need to pen off the more timid members of the flock for separate feeding so again, ensure you have the space available if you need to do this. The last thing you want is ewes losing condition at a time when their lambs are making their most rapid growth.

You also need to make provision for bonding pens for when the lambs arrive. We made these from temporary hurdles erected as and when needed around the edges of the barn. You can buy these commercially, but if you are handy with a hammer and nails you can soon knock up a few from various bits and pieces of wood lying around the farm.

We made hurdles from pallets, (usually too heavy for my taste, but the men thought them very robust) and from wooden trellising which had outlived its usefulness in the garden. These hurdles were very good, being light and easily erected and dismantled. We used the ubiquitous baler twine to tie them together. You can also buy woven hurdles made by coppicers. Again these are excellent, but tend to be expensive as most are destined for garden centres. Metal hurdles which will last a very long time are available from farmers' merchants.

Disease

Provided your building is well ventilated you shouldn't be troubled with pneumonia or other respiratory diseases, but there are other problems that may arise. Sheep are not really intended to be kept under intensive conditions which is what happens when they are brought inside.

Foot rot, always the shepherd's bane, is often cited as the chief bugbear of housed sheep and it's odds on that you will see at least one case of this during the winter months. Keeping a good bed of clean, dry straw will help a lot, but after several weeks of confinement the chances of an outbreak are greatly increased.

Housing

Good management will keep things under control and we kept outbreaks down by ensuring that the flock went on a foot rot vaccination programme. This was one of the best decisions we made as, in spite regular foot bathing and rotating pastures, we continued to suffer persistent outbreaks. Your vet will help arrange a suitable programme or you can simply follow the advice from the vaccine manufacturers as we did. If you are organic, of course, you will have to adopt different methods so you'll need to consult one of the organic organisations such as the Soil Association.

All feet should be trimmed before housing and if you use a foot bath, running them through this is a good idea. It goes without saying that infected animals should be treated. It can be a hard decision to make, but persistent offenders really ought to be culled from the flock as once the disease becomes chronic you never really get rid of it and they keep re-infecting other flock members. We also noticed that it tended to be hereditary so another good reason to move them on.

Preparation For Bringing Them In

When preparing the barn for housing we begin by putting down a thick base of wood chippings which we have in abundance as our son has a tree surgery business and these come free of charge. These chippings make an excellent base which seems to act as a filter, soaking up the wet and keeping the straw covering drier for longer. We use it with the cattle as well and have so far been well pleased with the results.

Showing Sheep

On top of the chippings we add a thick layer of straw. Barley straw is very palatable so we try to use wheat straw first as sheep are not so keen on eating this, but in reality either will do as the choice is really dictated by availability.

Foot rot isn't the only disease that can build up in housed conditions. A building that is repeatedly used each year can retain infections from previous years resulting in outbreaks of joint ill, a disease that affects new born lambs and, even more horrific, abortion storm which spreads very rapidly from one pregnant ewe to another causing them to cast their lambs before term.

Prevention is always better than cure, so to avoid these horrors you need to pay close attention to cleanliness. After turn out the building should be cleaned out as soon as possible and the walls and floor hosed down with a good quality disinfectant. Troughs and hurdles should get the same treatment. Everything, including the building itself, should be left empty for six months if possible.

This should ensure that you start with a "clean slate" when you bring in the flock. Worming the ewes, attending to their feet and administering the clostridial vaccines should complete the process.

Shearing

British winters can be exceptionally mild which means sheep kept in deeply strawed buildings can become uncomfortably hot, especially when heavily pregnant. For this reason many shepherds winter shear. We didn't do this as our flock was small and each ewe had plenty of space with a good air flow. Also, we rarely showed adult sheep except on a couple of occasions when we ended up lambing very late one year due to an infertile stock ram. This resulted in us having to keep that year's crop of ram lambs and run them on to shearlings. In that instance we had the whole flock sheared at the end of December.

If you intend showing adult stock you will probably need to winter shear so that they have a decent amount of wool growth for the summer show circuit. You can show them in their "working clothes," but you may find that they don't stand out as well as their more well groomed cousins. Unless, of course, your breed is always shown this way! Suffolks and many other lowland breeds are usually trimmed so winter shearing, for adult show stock at least, is usually carried out. Having said that, the way sheep are presented seems to be subject to fashion. During our show days you rarely saw an untrimmed Suffolk, never mind one taking the top prizes. Re-visiting the sheep show rings while researching this book I was quite surprised to find that classes for untrimmed sheep were now usual and at one show an untrimmed ram lamb took the Breed Championship.

There are other advantages to winter shearing as well as those of a purely cosmetic nature. You can get a higher stocking rate of up to 30% more from sheared ewes than those in the fleece as they will take up less room. Also, it is easier to spot a ewe failing in condition when sheared as

Showing Sheep

her back bone will be more easily visible. Some shepherds maintain that winter shorn ewes also give more milk. I can't vouch for this myself, but certainly it is easier for lambs to find teats when not obscured by long hanks of wool. During a mild winter, shorn ewes suffer less stress from heat than their woolly counterparts. They may consume more feed which in turn could result in heavier lambs. (I'm not sure if this is an advantage as bigger lambs can equal lambing problems, but the idea is that a big lamb is off to a flying start and will make a big sheep).

In case you're still worried about shearing in the depths of winter when a couple of feet of snow may be on the ground, be reassured. As long as your building is well strawed, draught free and out of the rain they will be fine. Do remember though, you should not turn out the ewes to grass for at least 8 weeks. In view of this, the best time for winter shearing is January, which will then coincide with spring turn out.

One note of caution! Heavily pregnant ewes should be handled with care. If you do winter shear, don't leave it too near to lambing and be very sympathetic in your handling. It is also not a good idea to winter shear ewes in poor condition or any over five years old.

Chapter Five
Halter Training

This might seem a bit daunting at first as the natural way of moving a sheep around is by driving within a flock and not by teaching it to walk quietly at your side on the end of a rope. Fortunately sheep, in spite of their somewhat skittish ways, are quite amenable to this type of handling and most soon get used to the experience.

To have a real chance of winning a prize you do need to start halter training early as it is important that your charge stands quietly and correctly in the ring and submits itself to a judge's inspection without any impressive gymnastic displays.

You also need to keep in mind that your show

Showing Sheep

stock not only has to lead nicely from a halter, but has to do this in front of dozens of spectators and other exhibitors to say nothing of a possible funfair, army shooting range, steam engine or the imagined delights of the neighbouring sheep lines. Without proper halter training, putting yourself and stock in this situation could well end in an ignominious retreat behind a bolting animal hell bent on demolishing ropes, tents, judges and spectators alike.

The best way of avoiding problems like these is to begin halter training your show stock about six weeks before the first event. Halters can be home made from soft rope or you can buy leather or rope ones. Your breed society may have some in stock or you should be able to get them from specialist or farm suppliers. A list is included in the suppliers section.

Use old or home made ones for training purposes and keep your new ones for the ring. A soft, white halter really sets off a black headed sheep, but many shepherds prefer leather as these have less of a tendency to cut. Some are furnished with brass fittings and can certainly emphasise the class of a quality animal. By the way, if you have a particularly wild animal and the halter starts to rub, you can make a very soft one with old woollen socks or binding with some soft cloth until the animal has calmed enough to revert to more traditional attire.

Halter Training

Fitting

Allow yourself plenty of time when you first introduce the halter as there is bound to be some resistance. Start by gently fitting the halter around the nose and behind the ears. It should fit snugly, but not too tight. It is very easy to fit a rope halter the wrong way around which means it will not slacken easily and could restrict breathing. It should tighten by pulling on the rope from UNDER the jaw, not from the top. If the lead rope comes from over the sheep's nose you have it the wrong way around.

You should use a quick release knot and never leave the animal unattended. Tie it to a strong rail or fence on a fairly short rope so that movement is restricted. Allowing a long length of rope is not only dangerous as the animal could become wrapped in the surplus, but also counter productive as being allowed to "fight" the halter will result in a longer period of acclimatisation.

About 15 minutes is long enough to start with. Only release the animal when calm. If the sheep shows little sign of settling but continues to struggle and fight as our big Suffolk ram lambs used to do on occasions, try offering a small feed. This usually calms them down, but it isn't good to make a regular habit of it otherwise they associate being tied up with eating and, instead of learning to stand still, will bunt at your hands and pockets. If you can repeat this process four or five times a day they will soon get used to the procedure.

Showing Sheep

Walking on

Once the sheep is happy standing you can then move on to walking. This often results in a lot of fun and games with the captive throwing itself forward and bolting for the nearest open gate. If like me you are not a candidate for a Wigan prop forward, you may find you need some help at this stage. We got around the bolting problem by cupping a hand under the sheep's jaw and keeping its head up. This will prevent it shooting forward, but you will still encounter some resistance so don't expect to solve the problem overnight. Patience and repetition are the keys. One trick that we tried with some success was to hold a bit of cake in the hand whilst holding up the head. It's amazing how greed can focus a sheep's mind.

The opposite of the bolting problem is pulling back. Strangely, few of our rams have ever done this, but you can usually encourage forward motion by having an assistant at the rear of the animal on the opposite side to the handler offering a little gentle encouragement. Alternatively you can try looping a piece of soft cord around the sheep's tail and using it to encourage forward movement. (Don't use a slip knot, otherwise it will tighten and you will cause a lot of pain and distress).

Before moving on to the next stage it's worth pointing out that spending time halter training lambs can pay big dividends when showing shearlings or adult sheep. I say this with the voice of experience. We have only shown shearlings infrequently due to the fact that during our showing years we rarely had any. This was because our lambs were born in January and sold during the autumn sales. One year, however, our stock ram went infertile with the result of having to get a late replacement. This had a knock on effect on lambing which took place in March/April.

The resulting lambs were not big enough for that year's sales so were kept over to the following year and sold as shearlings. Of course, by that time they were more than twice the size of the lambs we had previously been used to, which caused some major problems when it came to halter training.

The best ram, which was also the biggest, took great exception to having his head bound with a rope halter and reacted by bolting between my legs and carrying me, facing backwards, several hundred yards down a meadow until I eventually fell off, scratched and bruised in an ungainly heap at the bottom of a ditch. Had I been seriously injured I might have died from want of medical intervention since my husband and father were too helpless with laughter to administer first aid.

If that ram had been halter trained as a lamb, my dignity would not have suffered since even with a considerable lay-off, early halter training is well remembered and only needs a few "brush up" sessions.

Setting Up

When you have your sheep accepting the halter and walking forward without too much fuss, the next stage is to "set it up." This simply means getting it to stand so that it shows itself to its best advantage. If you have taught the animal to stand quietly it shouldn't be too difficult to do this.

Once you enter the ring you will be asked to stand in a line with your sheep at your side. It's quite in order to bend down and arrange the legs so that it stands nice and square, showing a long back to advantage. This will be helped by ensuring that the back legs are well apart. Take care that the rear legs do not extend unnaturally too far backwards, otherwise the rear end will look narrow and flat; not the effect you are trying to achieve. It will also slope the back which should look flat and broad, much like a billiard table. The sheep should give the appearance of having a "leg at each corner," something you will instantly recognise when you see it, but in cold print not the most helpful of graphics.

It is acceptable to put your hand under the chin to keep the head lifted and in the correct position and this also helps to control a restless animal that may get skittish at the unaccustomed noise and sights of the show. Many experienced shepherds will remain crouched, keeping one eye on their charge and the other on the judge until the awards are given out. Others, perhaps mindful of the strain on their backs, stand upright until nearer the time when the judge inspects their animal. The advantage of doing this is that you can gently step on a back foot should it creep forward and unobtrusively correct the animal's stance. Whatever you chose to do, be alert for instructions and concentrate on what is happening at all times. If you are gossiping to friends or family members outside the ring, most judges will give you very short shrift.

If your animal has caught the judge's eye you may be asked to parade it for further inspection. This is where good halter training will pay dividends. The judge has a much better chance of assessing the animal's qualities if it is not struggling and fighting its halter.

Even if you are still confined to ranks a well disciplined sheep at least shows that you understand the etiquette and principles of showing and will not cause complaint from your fellow exhibitors by possibly bowling them and their charges over as you bolt from the ring.

Chapter Six
Equipment

Make no mistake, trimming a sheep up to show standard, or even just doing some basic tidying up for a local sale not only involves a high degree of skill, but is very hard work as I know to my cost. My first efforts at trimming resulted in a Neanderthal stance that lasted a week and arthritic fingers complete with blisters and minor cuts. Fortunately, you can reap the benefit of my learning curve which begins by having the right equipment. This will go a long way to making the task easier, so let's take a look at what you'll need.

Equipment

Shears

Obviously an essential part of any shepherd's toolkit. You'll probably need to try out two or three different kinds before settling on a favourite. At first glance there seems to be little difference between them, but the small discrepancies can make a huge difference to how they operate and ease of use.

For instance, you can get single or double bowed hand shears. Both will do the job well, but the double bow variety are much easier to use and far less tiring than the single variety. When we started with our sheep we were given some equipment that contained an old pair of dagging shears which were fine for trimming soiled wool from around vents etc, but were murder to use for full scale clipping. They were very rusty as well, which didn't help matters.

Recently new scissor type shears have come onto the market, although I'm told they've been available in Europe for some time. I got the opportunity to test a pair and found them much easier to use than the traditional variety. They are spring loaded, light and very, very sharp.

Shears also come with different blade lengths, curved or straight blades and some are even designed for left handers, so if you can find a stockist with a range to try out it's worth spending some time getting a feel for what is comfortable.

Whatever you settle for you need to look after them properly by keeping them well oiled and carefully wrapped when not in use. If you can keep a separate pair for show preparation and use another set for general work that would also be a good option.

It should go without saying that shears must be kept sharp, but strangely enough, it is easy to overlook this. Personally, I was never very good at this technicality so used to get someone of a more practical bent to do the job for me. This worked fine, but I tended to forget that they would need re-sharpening every now and then and wondered why things were getting difficult. The moral of this little anecdote is to learn how to sharpen your tools yourself and keep a good sharpener handy!

You will also need a set of foot trimming shears. These are very different from dagging shears as the blade is much shorter and designed to trim back the hoof. Sheep, as you will probably know to your cost, can suffer greatly from foot problems of one sort or another, so it is important to keep the feet in good condition with regular trimming. This is even more so for show stock as lame animals don't win prizes.

Carding Combs

Next you'll need a special carding comb. You might have seen those used by hand spinners which consist of a flat board complete with blunted wire "teeth" used to tease the wool before spinning. You can opt for one of these if you wish, but a proper sheep carder is much better and makes the process easier.

Equipment

This consists of fabric backed with pointed teeth and sits on a curved, wooden block that easily allows the shepherd to use an upward, backward motion to fluff up the wool prior to trimming. At one time you had to make these yourself, but now they are readily available through various farm supplies outlets which also stock replacement wire for when you need to renew.

Carding Comb Cleaners

Carders tend to get bunged up with wool quite quickly so you'll need something to remove this. I generally used a horse's mane comb with good results, but also tried, with varying success, a variety of other long toothed implements found lying around the yard, most of which seemed to have dropped off various redundant agricultural implements.

Water Brush or Sprayer

The fleece needs to be dampened before carding and this is best done with a water brush as you need to get the water to penetrate a little. A sprayer will do the job, but as the water is applied as a mist you'll need to work it in with your hands, so go for a brush if possible and cut out the extra step.

Halters

By the time you reach the trimming stage your rising star should be perfectly at home in a halter. If not then now is not the time to practice your coiffeur skills! Go back to the halter training chapter as the animal must stand quite still while trimming is in progress.

Once this stage is reached you'll need several halters. The ones used for preparation need not be anything special as long as they do the job of restraining the animal, but show ones deserve more consideration. White rope sets off a black head to advantage, is not too expensive to buy but also has the advantage of being downgraded to general use when it has lost its pristine look. On the other hand, if your stock warrant it, a leather halter with smart brass fittings can add an extra touch of class. On the downside, these are much more expensive and require periodic cleaning.

Trimming Stands

Expert trimmers can often trim a lamb without the aid of a stand simply by using a halter and holding the sheep's head across an arm. Lesser mortals like me, who I suspect belong to the majority, make good use of a trimming stand.

At their most basic these consist of just a head restraint which fits under the chin with a rope going around the back of the ears. The contraption is bolted onto a hurdle or secure fence which renders the animal immobile.

The problem with devices of this sort is they keep the animal at ground level which means you spend hours crouched or squatting, hence the Neanderthal posture! I eventually solved this to some extent by raising the victim onto a platform, but the good news is that you can get trimming stands that already incorporate this feature. In fact, some are so sophisticated that they include a ramp which then raises the sheep to the correct height.

The above are what I would consider the essentials for show preparation. The following items some might also consider vital, but you may possibly get away with not using them or using alternatives.

Shampoos

Before trimming can begin you need to start with a clean fleece. I have to confess that we tended to use washing up liquid or cheapo shampoo from the local supermarket. You might prefer to use a specialist showing shampoo which come in several different flavours including ones for enhancing natural colour, e.g. the white of a Texel.

Rugs

A lot of shepherds keep their newly trimmed animals indoors on good straw beds until show time to avoid the risk of them getting dirty. We have never done this as our rams were destined to do a job of work, i.e. serve a flock of ewes during the variable days of autumn. We felt keeping them penned up would make them fat and unfit so they were always turned out into small paddocks unless the weather really was abysmal.

To keep the fleece clean they wore light rugs generally made out of old curtains or duvet covers. Many is the passerby who has done a double take when seeing three or four hefty ram lambs sporting floral jackets splashed with sprays of tea-roses. If you can't stand this type of embarrassment you'll

Showing Sheep

be glad to know that more professional rugs are available commercially. These are made of cotton or synthetic fabrics, are very light, durable and come in a variety of eye catching colours. You can even get them printed with your flock name if you want to go the whole hog.

Stain Remover

Beauty, they say, is in the eye of the beholder, which doesn't apply to sheep. In spite of your best efforts, inevitably at some time or other one of them (probably your best!) will manage to sit in something nasty. Having a bottle of stain remover handy can avert disaster. This stuff is easy to use. Just wipe it on, work up a lather and wipe off with a dry cloth. A bit like carpet mousse, come to think of it!

Pen Sheets

Show pens are usually constructed from metal or wooden poles and rails and do not restrict animals from "talking" to each other through the gaps. Unfortunately more than just ovine chatter can be transmitted by allowing this kind of access. The last thing you want is a scouring neighbour shooting its problems into or onto your stock. Using pen sheets will eradicate this hazard. You can make your own from redundant bed sheets or sacking, but the smarter option is available commercially in the form of nylon or plastic mesh, available in a variety of colours.

Grooming Oil

It is customary to brush the heads and feet of

black faced sheep with oil. This makes the black points shine and stand out. We used baby oil but, as you might have guessed, you can get specialist formulas to do the same job.

Show Bloom

Some shepherds like to colour the fleece when showing, even those that have naturally white wool. You can do this by using a brown show bloom. The stronger you make the solution, the darker the colour. Depending on strength, it fades within three months or it can be washed out with ordinary soap and water if you want to get rid of it earlier.

White Coats

These should probably be in the essential list as you will certainly need a clean white coat to do your exhibit justice when you enter the ring. Make sure that it has at least one pocket which you'll hopefully need for the rosettes. If not, then at the very least you'll want to keep your show schedule to hand.

Gentlemen, you will also need a tie. If you don't wear one you probably won't get penalised, but certainly, at the bigger shows it is expected and it won't do you any harm if you are seen to conform. You might also need a hat as it can get very hot at agricultural shows in spite of the vagaries of our weather.

Buckets & Bowls

It may sound rather obvious, but you will need

to supply your stock's own drinking and eating vessels.

Container

As you can see we've developed quite a list. Keeping this together in some kind of lockable container will help you avoid leaving anything vital at home. It also makes a good seat or picnic table.

Feed

Most shows, even small ones, usually provide some feed in the form of hay, but you will of course be feeding concentrates and other types of feed. This needs to be brought with you, especially if you're feeding cabbage as you are unlikely to get this on site. We always took our own hay as well as you can't always count on the organisers being particular with regard to quality or even quantity. You shouldn't need to have to supply bedding.

Flock Boards & other literature

These are simply a way of advertising your flock and letting potential customers see your contact details at a glance. They aren't essential, but are definitely a good idea as they help to present a professional approach. Adorned with rosettes or certificates they can do much to boost your standing as a breeder. You can make your own, but professionally made ones certainly look better and are not as expensive as you might think. Either way, include the name of your flock and full contact details including your address. If you have a website, add that as well.

Equipment

If you can afford to have some professionally produced leaflets containing information about you
and your flock printed, these are ideal for handing
to visitors to your pens. If funds are short you can
produce your own from any desktop publishing
software and run a few off as and when needed.

Most of the items listed in this chapter are available
through farm suppliers. Some may need to be
ordered and choice might be limited. You may
also be able to source some items at the shows
themselves, especially the breed stands. If you've
web access a quick search should provide a good
list of stockists, many of which you'll find in the
appendices at the back of this book.

Chapter Seven
Early Preparations

Take a close look at most show schedules and you'll see that there is nothing in the rules to say that you need do anything to your stock other than present it in a sound and healthy condition. In fact, some classes may stipulate that the animal is shown "in the wool," which means trimming, apart from squaring off the tail, isn't allowed, so why go to all the trouble of washing, carding and trimming?

That is a good question and one I have asked on many occasions, usually after a back breaking session with the trimming shears. As far as I can tell, it seems to have more to do with tradition than anything else, although some shepherds maintain that trimming and packing the wool helps a judge to examine the body more easily and check conformation. Others say that careful trimming can make a good animal that bit better or an inferior one less of a dud. How much truth there is in these statements is open to debate as judges are usually drawn from the ranks of exhibitors and are well aware of the "tricks of the trade." What is certain is that the majority of show sheep do receive some form of pre-show preparation and in many cases this is quite extensive.

Before discussing this in detail it would be a good idea to check with your particular breed society as to how your breed is shown. The following notes are aimed at short wool breeds, in particular Suffolks. Long wool varieties are not clipped in the same way as the staple type and length of their wool is an important part of their breed standard.

Shearing

For adult sheep the process begins well before the show circuit commences with shearing on or soon after 1st January. Actually many commercial flocks who house during the winter or lambing period do this as a matter of routine as it reduces stress caused by excessive heat which can build up when sheep are closely confined.

If you shear at this time you won't be able to turn out during bad weather without offering some alternative protection such as rugging, so be prepared to keep housed for several weeks until wool growth re-establishes and the weather warms up.

Washing

Depending on where you live you may not have to wash the fleece, but here in the Midlands pollution has always left our sheep a much darker shade than their more remote cousins. Be warned! No matter how good your handling facilities and organisational ability, you will almost certainly get a soaking.

I have tried to lessen this by wearing over-trousers and a nylon anorak, not a pleasant combination on a hot day, but even with this armour in place I have usually managed to get a fair amount of dirty water down my wellies.

Ideally you should aim to wash 2-3 weeks before the show. How you actually do this will depend on what you have available. We came by a very large, ex-fruit juice barrel that we sawed length ways. Wedged with bricks to stop it rocking and filled with warm water this made a reasonable shallow bath in which the animal stood. The head was secured by a restraint and it was then a simple matter of pouring over the water and working up a lather. Well, in theory! The reality was somewhat different. Most of the rams we showed were immediately suspicious of the bath. Convinced they were going to be drowned they usually jammed their front feet into the ground and refused to move. It would take at least two of us to more or less hoist them into the bath accompanied by much kicking, baaing and frantic scrabbling of hooves. During this process the barrel would often get turned over with most of its contents deposited on us. There would then be another fight to get the head into the restraint and a further bout of furious kicking before our victim was ready to give up. By this time I was usually soaked and exhausted and the sheep was as dirty as ever. (Hope I'm not putting you off!).

An alternative method we have used that was considerably less stressful to all concerned but more labour intensive is the tie-up and bucket method. This simply means securing the sheep in the head restraint and using buckets of clean water to wet and rinse the fleece. As you can imagine this tends to prove very tiring and laborious since it necessitates the continuous fetching and carrying of buckets of warm water.

If you or your sheep don't mind cold water you can use a hose pipe. Either way, you need to get the fleece well wetted. Once this is done wash thoroughly with gentle soap. We have generally used Fairy liquid, but there are specialist sheep shampoos on the market that you might like to try. You might also like to add some show dip to your water. No matter how gentle the shampoo, natural oils in the fleece will be destroyed. Adding some show dip will help to restore some body and, since some contain insecticides as well, the threat of fly strike is lessened.

You can also colour the fleece at this stage, although I don't mean in fluorescent pinks and yellows. Suffolks are often dyed a smart biscuit/beige colour and other breeds have their fleeces

Showing Sheep

whitened. This dye is usually applied by mixing in a watering can, pouring over the fleece and working in. The darker the colour, the more dye that needs to be added. It generally lasts about 8-12 weeks and can be washed out if desired.

It takes quite a while to work up a good lather which needs to penetrate right down into the fleece. Keep away from the eyes, mouth and nose and rinse very thoroughly.

Large rams will need a great deal of soap applying which in turn takes a lot of getting rid of. The best way to do this is to rinse several times with warm water, then switch to cold. The cold water seems to kill off the soap much quicker, especially after the initial warm water rinse.

At this stage you may be tempted to house until the wool has completely dried out. You should avoid doing this if it is possible as confining in a closed area when very wet may lead to respiratory problems or even pneumonia. The best option is to wash on a warm, sunny day and turn out into a clean paddock.

Don't worry if rubbing marks and grass stains appear. These will be addressed when the animal is trimmed.

Chapter Eight
Carding and Clipping

After all those months of careful feeding and constant attention I have always thought of the actual show preparation as putting the icing on a cake and, like anything of an artistic nature, it requires a fair degree of skill to make a proper job of it.

Although the following notes and photographs will help you will learn far more and at a lot quicker pace if you can find someone to actually show you how it is done. This shouldn't be too difficult as most breed societies keep lists of their members and should be able to put you in touch with someone in your locality. In fact, the

Showing Sheep

Suffolk Sheep Society organise occasional show preparation days for newcomers, so it's likely other societies do the same. Don't forget methods can vary between individuals and most definitely between breeds so, if in doubt check.

Speaking personally, I was first shown how to clip a ram lamb by Mr. Tom Harding, owner of the Bentley Flock of Suffolks. His son, Charles, is now President of the Suffolk Sheep Society and the Bentley flock was and still is one of the foremost flocks in the country. I considered myself very fortunate in getting such expert advice. The time I spent watching was worth its weight in gold, so I cannot emphasise enough the benefit of soliciting the expertise of a specialist breed expert.

This was further brought home to me when sourcing the photographs on the following pages. Mr David Inman of the Lindum flock kindly agreed to allow me to photograph him trimming a young ewe lamb. Within little more than an hour he had transformed the woolly fuzz ball into a sleek and elegant aristocrat fit for any show ring. Beginners will need to allow a little more time than this.

Be Patient!

This isn't a job you can hurry so the first thing you must do is ensure you have allowed plenty of time before the show. The process cannot be completed in one session so it is best to allow at least three days. If the show is on a Saturday we would start preparation on the proceeding Monday. You might need to allow more time while you are learning.

You'll also need to keep the animal still. This is vital, otherwise you could end up making some very drastic cuts which will effectively ruin the fleece for the season. Tie up with a halter if you must, but a proper trimming stand is best and well worth the outlay. Sheep seem much more resigned to their fate when put in these and will re-

main immobile for a considerable time, although it isn't really fair to keep them fastened in this way for longer than a couple of hours.

Positioning is also important. You need to have decent lighting so a dimly lit shed isn't a good idea, but neither is the yard in bright sun-light. I did my first lamb in this situation and ended up with sunburn and a sick headache!

Carding

This is the first part of the trimming process, although a lot of people like to cut the back out first (see photos). You need to spend some time doing this, probably as much as half an hour or more for a big shearling. A good carding brush is a must and it should have a curved back. This is to en-

Showing Sheep

able you to fluff up the wool with a quick backward flick of the wrist. Putting this action into words isn't easy, but it is very simple to do and will be immediately obvious when demonstrated (another good reason to find someone to watch!).

The aim is to create the "big hair" look that you see sported by Jimi Hendrix. You get results very quickly but it is easy to just card the surface wool. You have to remember to get all the twists and knots out, so you will have to go quite deep. If you don't do this stage properly you won't get the smooth, packed finish that you are aiming for. The back of a Suffolk should look like a smooth, level billiard table.

Before attempting to card, dampen the fleece well by spraying. You'll need to work it into the fleece as the droplets tend to stay on the surface. Repeat this as required while carding.

Keep 'em sharp!

Before even attempting to trim, make sure that your shears are really sharp. Trimming is a tiring enough job without having to contend with blunt shears which won't make a proper job of it anyway. You should also ensure that they are in good condition with the blades sliding over each other smoothly and level. Keep them well oiled when not in use and wrapped in an oily rag.

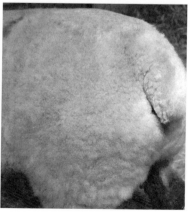

We have always sharpened our shears

Showing Sheep

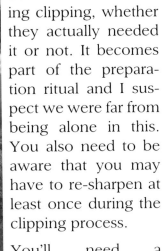

before commencing clipping, whether they actually needed it or not. It becomes part of the preparation ritual and I suspect we were far from being alone in this. You also need to be aware that you may have to re-sharpen at least once during the clipping process.

You'll need a sharpening stone to hone the blades. Hold this at an angle and apply to the bevelled edge. Be very careful not to stretch the spring.

It's worth pointing out that clipping shears work in a rather special way. The lower blade needs to be held flat and still with the upper blade being worked over it. It requires some practice to get the knack and is very tiring when you first begin. Make sure you have the double bow variety of shears as these are easier to use than the single variety.

There is also a scissor type of shears on the market now which are used extensively on the Continent. I recently saw these tested by a commercial shepherd who used them to hand shear a ewe. They were very, very sharp, but also much easier to hold and handle than the traditional shears. I can't vouch for how good they would be for show trimming, but their lightness and ease of use would certainly make them worth a try.

Think In Sections

Faced with a big hefty ram lamb with its wool standing on end like some kind of African witch doctor can prove a daunting task for a beginner who has never done anything more adventurous with a pair of shears than hacking off soiled wool. For this reason it helps to divide the task into sections.

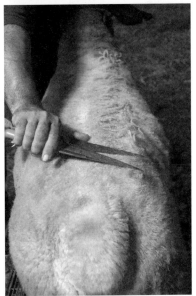

The Back

You could, if you wished, confine trimming to just

Showing Sheep

this area. We nearly always did this for animals destined for the autumn ram sales. If you are going to do this, don't card the rest of the animal.

You are aiming for a nice level back that accentuates the width and length of the animal. By the time you have finished the sheep will look "wedged," not rounded which is to be avoided at all costs.

Begin by making two parallel cuts from behind the ears, finishing just before the tail, but don't slope. Keep the cuts flat. You should now have a wide strip running the whole length of the back. Card this up and begin trimming away the fluff.

Start behind the ears and snip very slowly, moving forward by about 1cm at a time. Don't forget, keep the shears flat and level with the top blade moving over the bottom and, before you start, spray with water.

When you get to the hips, stop! Don't be tempted to follow the contours of the body, otherwise you will get a rounded shape which isn't what you are after. Turn around and go back up the other side and finish where you started, just behind the ears.

In all probability you'll find yourself doing these cuts several times if you are anything like me when I first started, as I was terrified of taking too much off. Perseverance does pay off, however, and the more you do it, the better and quicker you get.

Chest

Compared to the back this is a relatively small area, but you still need to be very careful. You'll have to take the sheep out of the trimming stand to do this and hold it by its halter. Stand over the sheep and hold up the head. Trim with small movements down to the bottom of the breast bone and

square this off with a nice, flat line. Once you are satisfied with this you'll need to do the sides of the neck which should extend from just below the ears down the front of the shoulders, ending in front of the legs, trimming off any wool inside these.

Only bend the head and neck slightly or you might take too much off. Keep the fleece damp by spraying and check your shears are still sharp.

Buttocks

You can put the animal back in the trimming stand to do this. Judges, and more importantly

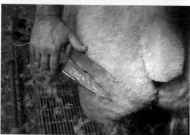

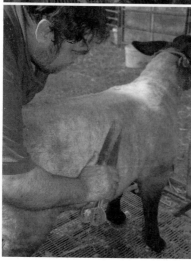

buyers, like to see a good, broad rear end, so try to keep this in mind when you begin to trim. Again, stand over the sheep and begin with the tail, trimming straight down the middle and finish with a nice flat line with no ragged wool trailing.

Still holding the shears vertically, continue down the sides of the tail. You are trying to achieve a flat, broad surface that ends in a straight line above the hocks. As with the front legs, trim off any wool from inside the legs and tidy up the wool on the scrotum of rams.

Sides

Hopefully it will be obvious what you need to do at this stage. The back, chest and buttocks should all be nicely trimmed and flat, so it is a case of trimming back the sides to join them all together. You can start from either the front or the back, the important thing is to keep the fleece damp and the shears flat. By this stage you should have got rid of the "Afro" look and hopefully achieved the box like shape which is the whole point of the exercise.

Not Finished Yet!

If you are thinking that it's time to stand back and admire your handy work, then you'll have to think again. We are not finished yet as the final stage of the trimming process is what some people call "facing" and puts the finishing touches to the fleece.

You do this by spraying again and carding as previously ex-

Showing Sheep

plained. This should produce a soft fluff which needs trimming off, but be very careful not to lose the flat, wedge-like shape you've just created.

You may need to do this a couple of times more. Each time there should be less fluff to take off. Pad down afterwards with something flat and fairly weighty like a small block of wood.

Show Dip

Depending on the breed, many shepherds spray with a show dip as this really puts a nice finish on the fleece. You will need to check this carefully though as different breeds need different colours. Suffolks, for example, are usually sprayed with a biscuit coloured dip. This is quite dark when it first goes on but lightens to the desired shade by the time show day comes around.

Keep it Clean

Having got your potential show champion in his best clothes it's vital you keep him clean for the big day. Some people confine to barracks on deep beds of fresh straw for the whole of the show season but we have only ever kept our animals inside during the two or three days preceding the show and, if the weather was good, then not at all. In this case we'd use rugs and clean paddocks. The rugs should be light and easy to fit and will keep the worst of the marks at bay, but even so,

don't risk granting access to muddy patches or turn out if the weather is really atrocious.

The Head

Although heads are often viewed as of little importance in a show animal this isn't really true as the size and shape of the head do play a part in ease of lambing and are included in most breed standards but, compared to other areas of the sheep, the head is way down on the scale of importance.

This doesn't mean you can forget about it altogether. Suffolk sheep, for instance, have jet black heads and shouldn't have any white hair present. Any that you come across need plucking out, or dare I say it, disguising. You can get a specialist preparation to do this.

On the day of the show rub over with a little oil, being careful not to get it in the eyes, nose, or mouth. Legs and hooves can also be treated in the same way. It goes without saying that these should be clean, properly trimmed and sound.

The above notes apply specifically to Suffolk sheep as this is the breed I'm most familiar with. The process is, however, similar for most of the down breeds, but do check with the breed societies for any variations. I've also included some short notes on other breeds, but please use these as a starting point and contact the appropriate breed society for more details as some do run training courses and offer pamphlets and videos.

Non-Down Breeds

Many of these are shown in their natural state so the only preparation that is allowed is the removal of soiled wool and other debris so it is vital you check with your particular breed society to find out what is and is not allowed.

Leicestershire Longwool

These magnificent looking animals do receive preparation prior to showing which was kindly explained to me by Mr. Barry Enderby, owner of the Delta Flock and secretary of the Leicester Longwool Sheep Breeders Association. As far as I am aware, the notes below apply to all the Longwools, but do check first.

The process starts about six weeks before the show by washing. It's important to do this early enough, otherwise you risk washing the lustre out of the fleece. Three weeks later a purl show dip is applied by hand, not by plunge dip. This helps to crimp the wool into curls. It's important to get this stage right by applying the correct strength of dip, otherwise you may end up with an orange sheep. To avoid this the dip is applied every two weeks starting with a weak strength and gradually increasing. If the weather is good the dip can be applied weekly.

Very little trimming is done except for tidying up the belly wool, squaring tails and removing whiskers from the face.

A few hours before the show the staples need to be separated out. This should be done by hand. A brush is never used.

Beltex

This is one of the main terminal sire producing breeds for crossing with commercial flocks. Its main characteristics are double-muscled hindquarters coupled with fine bones which ensures maximum killing-out percentages. It is a white fleeced, white faced sheep which is shown with a minimum of preparation. It is sheared in May and washed a few weeks before the show. No trimming is done, but efforts are made to keep clean by using sheets and keeping inside with regular access to clean paddocks.

Texel

Another of the popular terminal sires, the Texel is noted for its meat, not wool, so little emphasis is placed on wool preparation. It is sheared from May onwards and is shown naturally with no trimming or shaping, although you are allowed to wash and

Showing Sheep

use a show dip, hence the rather attractive biscuit colour you see at some shows.

Charollais

Yet another very popular terminal sire. Show preparation begins by shearing bare on or after 1st December, so you will need to keep them warm during the winter months. The breed society discourages shaved heads and encourages judges to discriminate against the practice.

Jacob

These are sheared early in the year so you must make sure they keep warm by feeding well and confining indoors until the weather warms up. Washing takes place anywhere between three weeks and a few days before the show using washing up liquid or animal shampoos. The wool is carded and it is often left at that for lambs. The adults usually get lightly trimmed, often the day before the show, and rugs provided to keep them clean. Faces and legs are checked prior to entering the ring and washed if needed. Horns are oiled to give a little shine.

Black Welsh Mountain

These are a neat little sheep noted for the colour and quality of their wool, which is very popular with hand spinners. It's shown with minimal preparation. Some people wash and lightly trim them but others just tidy them up prior to showing. Leaving them out to the weather causes the ends of the wool to take on a reddish appearance which I find quite attractive. If you don't like it you'll have to keep show stock indoors which rather defeats the object of keeping these sheep as they are noted for being extremely hardy conservation grazers.

Zwartbles

These attractive black sheep with white stockings and blaze originate from Holland and have a band of enthusiastic supporters. They are sheared after 1st January and may be lightly trimmed, although no attempt is made to produce the "box" shape of the Down breeds. The use of artificial colouring, paint, sprays or chalk to enhance or disguise white areas is not allowed. The ends of the wool bleach naturally to a reddish brown and this is permitted, although some breeders trim it off.

Obviously there are many more sheep breeds than those I've listed here, so if I haven't mentioned yours, don't despair! Almost all the breeds have their own society which you'll find in the Appendix. Do please contact the secretary for advice. They know their breed best and will be up to date with any rule changes that could affect the way stock is shown.

Finally, if you don't want to go to the trouble of trimming you probably don't have to. You will likely find that your breed society allows both trimmed and untrimmed sheep to be shown so again, check with your society. During the writing of this book I visited several shows that staged classes for both trimmed and untrimmed Suffolks and the untrimmed animal on occasion took the breed championship.

Chapter Nine
Show Schedules and Classes

One of the best things about showing is the variety and number of opportunities available to exhibit. The Royal Show, the Royal Highland, The Royal Welsh and The Balmoral in Northern Ireland as well as the bigger county shows may be initially out of your league, but there will be plenty of smaller shows and country fairs taking place throughout the summer where you stand a reasonable chance of getting among the ribbons. Particularly recommended are the shows put on by Smallholder Associations, especially if you keep rare or native breeds. These are very friendly events where people generally have the time to talk to a beginner. Many of our successes have been at these events and have been no less enjoyable for being of a more modest nature than the national venues.

Obviously distance and movement restrictions will play a part in how far you can travel, which may cut down your options somewhat, but you should be able to find some shows within your vicinity. If you haven't yet decided on a breed and really don't want long show journeys, it's worth researching the local breeds. Most local shows will stage classes for these as it is not an unreasonable assumption that they will be well supported by local stock.

Often breed society shows are held at open show venues such as County Shows with their classes running in conjunction with the open classes or they may be staged at a private venue open only to society members. If you join your particular breed society you should be kept well informed of all suitable show venues for your stock.

As for open shows, these are easy to find. The Resource chapter in this book lists some, plus an excellent website for finding more.

For many shepherds of rare and minority breeds the society shows will be the most attractive as it is difficult to compete against the more popular commercial breeds at the open shows when it comes to the top honours such as the interbreed championships.

Showing Sheep

How it all works

If you have never been involved with showing any form of livestock before you may be a little confused by the jargon at this point, so this is a good time to explain how it works.

You enter your sheep into the appropriate breed classes, but more on that in moment. This will be specifically for its breed or sometimes a class covering a group of similar breeds if entries are low. The animals are judged and rosettes awarded. The winners of all the breed classes will be invited to take part in a Breed Championship. For example, all the winners of the classes specifically for Jacob sheep will be judged against each other and a Breed Champion selected.

All the Breed Champions may then go forward to the Interbreed Championship. I say may because the larger shows often restrict which breeds to consider for the supreme Championship. Typically these will be all or some of the following: Suffolk, Wensleydale, Texel, British Charollais and Lleyn. Depending on size there is often a separate judge appointed to make these top awards.

Only two prizes are offered. Champion and Reserve Champion. These are the coveted awards to which most breeders aspire. Unfortunately, unless you own one of the popular commercial breeds such as those just mentioned, your chances of taking one of these prizes in the open competitions on the County Show circuit aren't very high. I've no doubt there are a few minority breed success stories out there, but this is why society shows are popular. The playing field is much more level with like competing against like. Providing your stock meets all its breed standards you have as much chance of carrying off the top awards as any other society member.

Having said this a lot of shows do offer other awards which give the minority breeds more of a chance of bigger prizes, but ultimately the one everyone would like to win is the Supreme Champion.

A final word on this section. The above is only a rough guide as schedules vary from show to show. Also, secretaries have to balance their books and, if entries are low, they will reserve the right to amalgamate classes which you may not be aware of until the day of the event.

Schedules

Most shows take place from about May onwards through to September. Schedules which list times, classes and rules are usually available from early spring. Many can be downloaded from the web along with entry forms, but if you're technologically challenged, show secretaries are still perfectly happy to send these by post.

The first thing to do is check that they are actually staging sheep classes. This may sound obvious but shows do change their policies and, with disease threats such as Foot and Mouth and Blue Tongue having major impacts on animal movement, classes can be cancelled at the last minute. I well remember confidently requesting the schedule for

Showing Sheep

a small country fair at which we had exhibited the previous year only to find they had discontinued the sheep classes after the big Foot and Mouth epidemic in 2001.

What classes are being staged will depend to some extent on size and which breeds are popular in the area. Organisers can reasonably expect that the local breeds will be prominent so will usually ensure there are plenty of classes for them. This isn't always the case so a careful perusal of the show schedule, especially if there is a clash of dates, is a must to maximise your opportunities of gaining a prize for your efforts.

Classes

Even if you are not familiar with showing you will probably have enough knowledge of sheep by now to understand most of the terms associated with the classes, but just to clarify I've set out a typical listing of classes that might be encountered at the average County show together with a few notes where things may not be very clear.

Suffolks (These are breed classes. If yours is a minority breed you may find it has been lumped in with other breeds).

Class

280   RAM, shearling or over (Will have been sheared at least once. Can be shown trimmed or untrimmed, but usually trimmed. The number is the Class number which you'll need to complete your entry form).

Getting your sheep used to the halter will make parading around the ring less stressful and help show your animal to advantage.

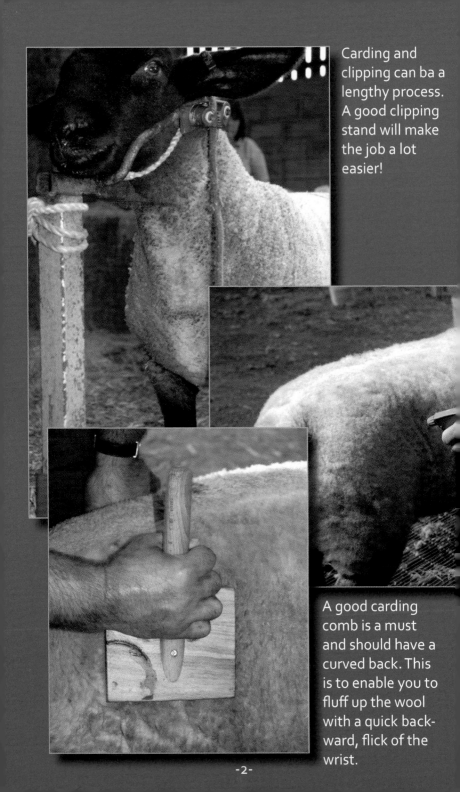

Carding and clipping can ba a lengthy process. A good clipping stand will make the job a lot easier!

A good carding comb is a must and should have a curved back. This is to enable you to fluff up the wool with a quick backward, flick of the wrist.

Use a smaller carding comb for the more delicate areas.

Spray the fleece throughout to keep it slightly moist - this makes it easier for carding and clipping.

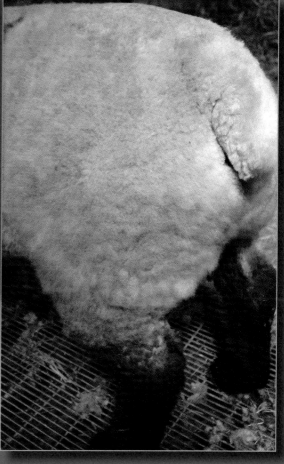

When finished carding a, Suffolk or any other Down breed, the back should be flat.

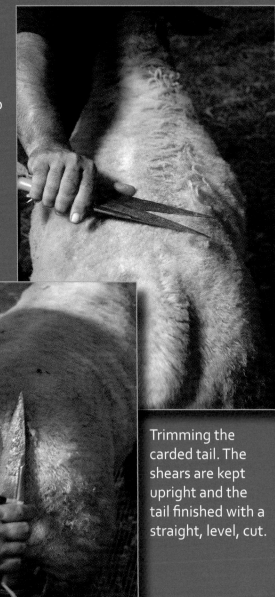

Trimming the carded back. Note how the shears are kept flat with the top blade moving over the bottom one which should remain still.

Trimming the carded tail. The shears are kept upright and the tail finished with a straight, level, cut.

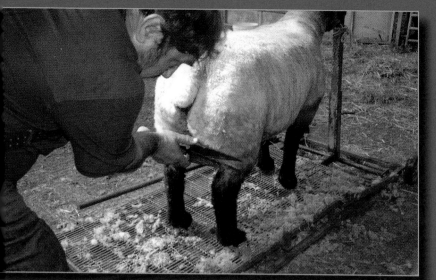

(Above) Trimming the carded buttocks. The aim here is to make
the rear end look as wide and full as possible. Don't forget to
clean up inside the legs.

(Below) When trimming the neck
don't over stretch otherwise you
may end up with an uneven trim.

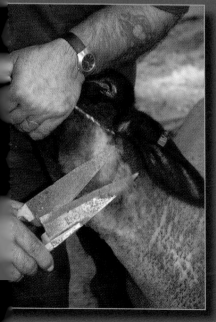

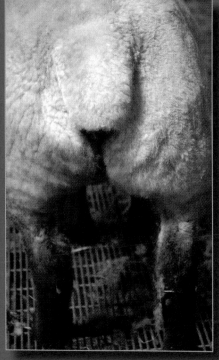

Note how the trimmed buttock
looks wider and bigger than the
carded, but un-trimmed side.

This judge is making a prelimary inspection for conformation and condition.

(Above) Teeth should line up properly and are always inspected.

(Left) Judges will pay a lot of attention to the rear end as broadness and depth will often carry the day.

All the sheep societies have their standards and will give ready advice on show preparation.

Some soceities permit coloured washes to be applied.

Whether it's a hobby or a commercial necessity, there is room for everyone on the show circuit.

(Above) Youngsters are particularly encouraged with most shows staging special classes for young handlers.
(Below) The 2008 Royal Show Suffolk Champion.

281   RAM LAMB (Born from the preceding December onwards and shown trimmed. If this was the only class for a Ram Lamb you would have the option of showing trimmed or un-trimmed).

282   UNTRIMMED RAM LAMB (No trimming allowed, just a squaring of the tail and a little tidying up. Soiled wool should be removed).

283   EWE that has suckled a lamb this season. (Can be any age).

284   GIMMER shearling (female sheep that has been sheared once).

285   EWE LAMB (female sheep that has been born from the preceding December. As this is the only class for Suffolk ewe lambs entries can be trimmed or un-trimmed. At the bigger shows they will mainly be trimmed).

286   GROUP OF THREE (one male any age and two females already entered in previous classes, to be owned and shown by one exhibitor or sometimes more than one exhibitor. The show schedule will make this clear).

There will of course be a similar set of classes for other breeds and each will be headed by details of who will be doing the judging, times and entry fees.

Prizes and Awards

Monetary awards are not great, £15, £10 & £5 being typical of quite large agricultural shows so few breeders expect to get rich on prize money alone. By far the most important prizes are the red

Showing Sheep

rosettes that you can add to your flock board and display to prospective purchasers at other shows and sales. If one of these is the Supreme Interbreed championship, then so much the better.

Trophies are also sometimes awarded but usually these have to be returned in time for next year's show, so if you do win one of these remember to keep it well polished.

Entry Forms

These are usually supplied with the schedule. They should be filled in and returned in good time as there is often a cut off date after which no further entries are accepted. Entry fees are payable, so make the secretary's job easier by ensuring you enclose the correct money and a stamped, addressed envelope if requested.

Other Forms and Documents

If you thought form filling stopped with the entry form it's time to think again. Moving animals off your holding is no longer the simple task it once was. The various documents you need to be familiar with are discussed in the Health & Welfare chapter.

Chapter Ten
The Big Day

The day of reckoning has finally arrived which will hopefully reward the months of care and attention lavished on your progeny. All being well, your star will be at least clean and presentable and a perfect picture of rude health. If you have elected to trim, hopefully you will have made a reasonable job of it. If you haven't, it is no good worrying about it at this stage. You may think your efforts are a complete disaster, but judges are selected for their experience and will see beyond any cosmetic mishaps, provided they are not too drastic.

It should be a day of excitement and one to enjoy, but for beginners it can often degenerate into one of hair tearing frustration so do as much as you

Showing Sheep

can in advance to minimise stress.

The Kit Box

It's amazing how much equipment you seem to need just to show even one sheep. To ensure you know where everything is, set yourself up with a good strong box (see 'container' P.68), preferably one that can be locked, and pack it the day before the show. You'll have your own ideas of what it should contain, but typically we would add as much of the following as would fit in. The rest would be stacked alongside so that everything was at least kept in the same place.

Trimming Kit

These are the tools used during the trimming procedure i.e. shears, carding combs and water spray, any of which might be necessary for some last minute tidying up. Stain remover is also a good idea. You will need some kind of oil too for applying to black heads and legs just before entering the ring. Proprietary ones are available, but we tended to use baby oil since there was always plenty of it available having young lambs of our own.

Halters

Leather ones should be well polished and white ones very clean and bright. Use new ones if the show is an especially important one.

Small First Aid Kit

Ours have usually contained foot trimming shears in case of sudden lameness, wound powder,

Dettol, green ointment (a very effective homemade remedy for open wounds made from comfrey and lavender) and antibiotic spray. If you do have to use this be very, very careful! It leaves bright blue stains which take weeks to fade.

Advertising Banners, Boards & Flyers

If you are just starting out you may not need these initially, but once you have established yourself they are a very good idea as they will help to create credibility and help sell your surplus stock.

Banners can be professionally created and should contain your flock name and contact details including a website if you have one. Many breeders like to incorporate a picture of their breed as well and some flock owners have pen sheets printed with their flock details too.

Display boards tend to be more popular than banners as they can be used for displaying rosettes which are the best form of advertising, especially if they happen to be red or have Inter Breed Champion written on them.

You might also like your board or boards to display some information about the breed, e.g. it might be particularly suited for smallholders wishing to supply organic meat. Alternatively you might like prospective purchasers to know that your animals thrive at a certain altitude which is a claim some lowland sheep breeders sometimes make.

As long as you are not making blatantly untrue claims there is no restriction on what you can say on your boards, so it makes good sense to use

Showing Sheep

them to advantage.

You can get flock boards professionally made but there is nothing to stop you making your own, providing you have a steady hand. There are a range of suitable materials around and the designs that people manage to come up with are many and varied to say the least.

Flyers

If you have access to a computer advertising flyers can be designed quickly and easily and run off as and when needed. If your skills are more practical than technical, then for a small outlay you can get the same job done at a copy shop. The last time I had black and white A5 flyers printed the cost was £25 for 1000.

You may be wondering why you need flyers at all. The answer is simply to make people aware of surplus stock you may have for sale and any other products, e.g. farm gate lamb, beef etc. Shows are not just places for showing off your animals and perhaps winning a prize or two, they should also be seen as a shop window for your other products.

Of course, if you don't have any surplus stock or anything to sell then flyers may not be necessary. Even so, it doesn't do any harm to have an eye to the future. Producing a flyer that says something about your breed and your farm that people can take away with them may elicit a call at some future date when you are thinking about reducing numbers.

If you are producing flyers, you will need a box to contain them. Perspex is best as people can easily see what they contain. Attach this to the pen in a prominent position.

Pen sheets

Not everyone uses these but they are a good idea as they will help keep your animals clean and might also stop infection if penned next to other sheep who may be brewing something nasty. You can buy commercial ones which look very smart as they come in several colours or you can make your own from sacking or recycled tarpaulin.

Rugs

These are a great help in keeping stock clean. You can make them yourself out of old bed sheets or duvet covers, perhaps avoiding flowery prints unless you want to raise a smile. Commercial ones are available and can be printed with your flock name and details.

White coats

When worrying about your protégés, it is easy to overlook your own appearance. There are certain expectations and conventions when showing stock and it may be frowned upon if you choose not to conform to these. A clean white coat is a must, and when we were showing men were expected to wear ties. This doesn't seem to be quite as true nowadays but gentlemen, at least at the bigger shows, should still dress for the occasion as it will help prove that you are taking things seriously. You might also want to wear a hat if it is very sunny as you could be out in the ring for quite a long time.

Buckets & Bowls

Shows do not supply feeding equipment so you will need to bring your own but water will be available. Don't forget to keep checking the buckets as sheep, when confined in a small pen, have a habit of fouling their water.

Feed & Bedding

Bedding is usually provided free of charge and sometimes hay, or it may be available for purchase. Green food is also sometimes available. It may have to be ordered in advance or it may be provided on a first come, first served basis. This may be stated on the show schedule, but you can always check with the organisers if in doubt. Along with many flock owners we have usually brought our own feed, mainly to avoid any risk of digestive upsets.

Trimming Stand

We never bothered taking this, but some people are happier knowing it is there if they want to use it. A head restraint which can be clamped to pen rails is usually sufficient for any last minute preparations.

Shepherd's Comfort

Although there will be plenty of refreshment outlets at the show these can be expensive, especially if you have a young family to provide for. If this is the case then don't forget your own food and drinks, plus soap and towel or baby wipes in case you need to clean up after handling stock. The latter also come in handy for younger members of the family after visits to the ice-cream van!

Paper Work

Unfortunately there is a fair bit of this and it is all vital. Schedules, numbers, movement licenses and health certificates all need to be kept easily to hand. The schedules will tell you when and where your class is due to take place, so keep it handy. The other paper work involved with moving and showing sheep is discussed in detail in Chapter 11. It is also important to check class times and dates! These are only approximate and it has been known for organisers of bigger shows to change dates of Championship classes from those printed in the schedule.

At the Show

Having loaded everything up and confident that your paper work is in order, it's now time to hit the road. Allow yourself plenty of time to reach your destination and be aware that traffic is likely to be heavy, especially as you approach the show ground. It is also a good idea to listen in on traffic reports so that you can avoid any likely black spots.

County shows tend to allocate different gates for exhibitors and public. You should have received details of which gate you are to use, so make sure you are aware of this well before you reach the show ground. Getting it wrong will not make you

Showing Sheep

popular with the gate stewards and could cause you a long delay through having to re-queue at the correct entrance.

Agricultural shows section livestock into species areas so you will be directed to the sheep section by a steward and allowed to unload. You will have been given pen numbers beforehand and these should be easily located.

You are not always able to park your vehicle near to the pens so this is where a good box comes in as it will reduce the amount of time needed to unload everything and lessen the risk of forgetting something which could entail a long walk back to the car park.

Be Alert!

If you have allowed yourself plenty of time you should be able to settle yourself and your animals into your allotted space in plenty of time before the judging commences. Any last minute preparations such as oiling heads and legs can be done and white coats donned without getting into a panic. Don't be too laid back, however, as you must be aware of when your class is being called.

Classes are scheduled to start at particular times and usually do begin on time. Unfortunately timing can soon go awry if one class takes longer to judge than expected. For this reason you must treat all class times as a guide and keep an eye on the ring stewards. These may come around the pens and call the class or check your presence, but don't rely on it. The ring steward's other job is to act as escort to the judge, so it is your responsibility to get yourself and your stock into the ring at the correct time. If someone has to come looking for you, you won't be very popular.

In the Ring

When you get to the ring you will probably be met by the ring steward who will ask for your number and mark you present, if he hasn't already done this. You are then asked to join the line of other exhibitors in the centre of the ring and may be put into numerical order, although smaller shows don't usually bother doing this.

Setting Up

Sheep in Britain are not usually paraded around the ring for any length of time, as most don't lead all that well. You will almost immediately be expected to form a line, so it is important to get your animal to show itself to its best advantage. This is called "setting up or stood out." If you have done your halter training well this isn't too difficult. Put your hand under the sheep's chin and lift the head so that it stands proud. This will also help to steady a nervous animal. Make sure each leg is straight and at each "corner." Try to emphasis a long back with width at the rear end, but don't encourage your charge to stand like some dogs are set up, with the hind legs exaggeratedly extended. This will cause the back to slope and the buttocks to flatten which, apart from looking ridiculous, isn't the effect you are after.

Being small animals sheep will result in you having

Showing Sheep

to do quite a lot of bending to get everything displayed to best advantage. Some people choose to crouch down and remain in this position while judging takes place. This is perfectly acceptable, but be careful not to get between your charge and the judge. Even if the judge is not actively examining your sheep he will often need to compare one or more animals as he makes his inspection. If you block his view you won't be doing yourself any favours.

In any case, when the judge first enters the ring he likes to take a careful look at the exhibits by walking up and down the line and examining them from the rear. While he is doing this it is a good idea to stand in front of your animal and face towards the judge.

Irrespective of how good or otherwise the exhibits are, all of them will be subject to an initial examination by the judge, so do everything you can to ensure your animal shows itself to its best advantage. Good halter training will really pay off at this stage as both handler and sheep could be faced with quite a long wait while all the entries are examined in turn.

You should also have got your sheep used to being handled by strangers as part of the judging process involves feeling the back, sides, chest and rear areas and the scrotum of rams and the udders of ewes and also checking the fleece. Nervous animals may object to this, making it very difficult for the judge to complete his examination.

He will also check the teeth either by looking

himself or asking you to open the mouth for him. Occasionally lambs are born with undershot or overshot jaws. These are very bad faults and, should you breed a lamb with these traits, you would be well advised to cull it from the flock as soon as you can. The teeth will also tell him that the animal does conform to its stated age.

Judges like to check for soundness so you might be asked to walk your charge up and down for him to check its gait, or he may ask the whole class to parade in a circle before he commences individual examinations. Alternately, entrants could be asked to release their animals and allow them to wander around the ring while the judge inspects them under a more natural setting. A small shedding pen is set up in the corner of the ring to help with recapturing if this is the favoured procedure. Different judges have their own preferences, so this is another reason for staying alert.

Don't Chat!

As already said, you will be faced with quite a long wait while the other exhibits are being judged. Don't start chatting with your neighbours except to exchange a polite word or two. The same goes for supporters outside the ring. Not only is it bad manners and shows that you are not taking proceedings seriously, but it can also be distracting for the judge. Your mind will also wander from your charge and animals, as we all know, can be quick to take advantage when attention is distracted.

Some judges can be very kindly and are often aware

Showing Sheep

of a newcomer's nervousness and may chat a little to try and put you at your ease. Don't take this as a license to get into a full blown conversation. Simply answer his questions and leave it at that. You will get the opportunity for a more lengthy discussion after the judging is completed.

Keep Watching!

When you have been showing for a while you will soon realise that you are in with a chance of a prize if the judge keeps casting a glance your way when examining the other animals. He is comparing qualities. If he keeps comparing your sheep with several others, the signs are good. Even if this doesn't happen, you should still be alert and keep your sheep displaying itself to its best advantage.

Quite often it is very difficult to choose between two or more animals. In this case the judge may move his favourites so that they are placed side by side for easier comparison at the top of the line. They may also be asked to walk out and there will almost certainly be a further brief physical examination.

The winner will be indicated by a short tap on the rump which is the signal for the ring steward to come forward to note down numbers and hand the rosettes to the judge for presenting.

When the Party's Over

If you have been awarded a rosette, please don't engage in theatrical displays of celebration and don't let your supporters outside the ring whoop and cheer either. Farming folk tend to be quite reserved, so a smile and a polite thank you should suffice. The judge will offer his congratulations as he hands you the rosette and may give some useful comments on your animal. Now judging has been completed it is fine to chat a little, but keep it pertinent and remember that some of the non-winners may also like to speak to him as well. He won't have a lot of time as he will have other classes to judge. If you are a breed winner you will also be called on to compete for the Breed Championship, so this still isn't the time to get too chatty.

Once More into the Fray!

When all the breed classes have been judged the winners will once again be called into the ring to compete for the Breed Championship and Reserve Championship. Depending on the size of the show there may also be other special prizes as well, but these will be detailed in the schedule. If the second place winner in a class is particularly good the judge may ask to see that animal again as well. If this is a bit mystifying it is because this animal, although it cannot be considered for the Championship, could possibly beat the first prize winners in the other classes and take the Reserve Championship. It isn't something that happens very often, but it has been known on occasions.

Having been awarded the Breed Championship, the coveted Interbreed Championship is within reach. Not all breeds are eligible for this as some of the big shows restrict this prize to the main

Showing Sheep

terminal sire producing breeds. Should you keep one of these you will be called into the ring for the final time. A new judge is often appointed to judge this one class which means he will be meeting the animals for the first time.

It's a very tense moment for all concerned and there are often a lot of spectators around the ring. If you are not involved in the judging but are watching, please don't engage in idle chatter. This is a golden opportunity to watch and learn without having the distraction of shepherding your own sheep. You will be looking at the best animals in the show, so try and see how they compare to yours.

When the award is made, applaud the decision. If you know the winner avoid congratulating him or her until they have been presented with their rosettes and any trophies. Also, it's likely that the press will want to take photographs so stay back until this has been done.

If you are the winner and have been descended upon by the rural paparazzi, make the most of it. They will want you to display your prize winner to best advantage, so co-operate with them as much as you can. It may take quite a while to get the photographs they are after, but it's to your advantage to go along with them. Likewise, make sure you are well versed in the animal's breeding and that of its parents as you will almost certainly be asked for details of these. This kind of publicity should be milked for all it is worth as it is just the kind of free advertising you need to help sell your surplus stock during the autumn sales.

What else?

If you are awarded a prize, put the rosette in your pocket rather than trying to fix it to the animal. When you return to your pen it can be transferred to your flock board if you have one, or fixed on to the pen rails.

Sportsmanship

Nobody likes losing but beginners will certainly have to learn to get used to it as it takes time to achieve success in the show ring, especially if you have to breed up stock to winning standards. Should you be an also ran, do be a good sport and give the winners a clap and a few words of congratulations. As for the judge, he is only human. Don't start arguing with him and don't storm off in a temper if you think he made a terrible mistake. You paid for his opinion and if you didn't like it, well there is always another day and another show.

Chapter Eleven
Rules, Regulations and Health

You had better take a deep breath before reading this chapter as it mainly concerns red tape. Sheep, unfortunately, are subject to quite a few diseases, some of which can spread with alarming rapidity, not only amongst the same species but also across to other kinds of livestock. Foot and Mouth and Blue Tongue are just two notable examples. These are notifiable diseases and are far from being the only ones. Others include Avian influenza, Classical Swine Fever, Newcastle disease, Anthrax, Aujeszky's disease, Bovine Spongiform Encephalopathy, Brucellosis, Enzootic Bovine Leukosis, Scrapie, Tuberculosis (Bovine TB) and Warble fly.

Fortunately, many of these are quite rare but you should still be aware of what they are and their typical symptoms. If you suspect any of your animals have a notifiable disease you must report your suspicions without delay to a DEFRA Divisional Veterinary Manager, contactable through your Local Authority, (England, Wales & Scotland), the Department of Agricultural and Rural Development, (Northern Ireland) or a member of the police force. I don't intend to cover all the notifiable diseases in the above list as some don't apply to sheep, but a quick reminder of the symptoms of both Foot & Mouth and Blue Tongue would be appropriate as these have had a major impact on farming during the recent past.

Foot & Mouth

Symptoms in sheep are rarely noticeable, but may include fever, severe lameness affecting one or more legs, a stiff-legged walk, a tendency to lie down or an unwillingness to rise, increased lamb mortality and a general look of being unwell. The disease is rarely fatal and will usually run its course within 2-3 weeks. As animals lose condition financial losses can be great, so control, at the time of writing, is through mass culling as evidenced in the 2001 outbreak. If there is a major outbreak of Foot & Mouth, there is a complete movement embargo and livestock classes at shows will be cancelled.

Blue Tongue

This hit our shores during the autumn of 2007, arriving from the Continent via infected midges. It is these insects that spread the virus. The main clinical signs are a persistent fever, lameness, a swelling of the face and a blue colouration of the tongue, lips and coronary band. Symptoms can vary in severity, depending on the strain of the virus and the breed of sheep. The mortality rate amongst sheep is very high. Fortunately, the disease can only be transmitted to sheep by biting midges and is not transmissible between sheep. There is now a vaccine available which all shepherds are strongly urged to use. For sheep just a single yearly dose is required.

Showing Sheep

How Does This Affect Showing?

Having learned a hard lesson during the 2001 Foot and Mouth outbreak, Defra has put some strict rules into practice in an effort to minimise the spread of disease by controlling animal movements. This means you cannot take stock back and forth across the country to shows and sales without complying with strict regulations.

The measures outlined here apply to England. There may be differences for Scotland, Ireland or Wales so, for the very latest information on animal movements, check with Defra or your local Animal Health Office.

Stand Still Rules

Once you have moved stock off your holding and then brought them back, all the sheep, cattle and goats on the holding must remain on the farm for the next 6 days or longer in the case of pigs. Obviously this can cause problems for breeders attending a lot of shows staged close together. Fortunately there are some exemptions which apply to shows, but to qualify you must follow certain procedures. Full details of these can be found by contacting Defra or your local Animal Health Office, but briefly:

1. You will need to individually identify all stock which you intend to show with appropriate ear tags.

2. A Defra approved isolation unit must be set up. This may be buildings or pasture, but needs to be physically separated by at least 3 metres

from buildings or pasture used by non-isolated animals. This unit needs to be approved by the Local Authority Animal Health Office.

Once approval is given show animals can be kept in this unit for six days and then taken to shows without triggering the stand still rule. As they are in isolation they do not trigger the stand still rule for the rest of the sheep, goats or cattle on the farm either, which means that animals destined for markets etc. are not affected by those going to shows.

Once the show season has finished the show stock can be returned to the main flock after completing a 6 day stand still in the isolation unit.

Double Tagging

All sheep born on or after 11th January 2008 must be doubled tagged if they are expected to be reared beyond 12 months of age or exported. Two tags can be used, or one tag and a tattoo. Eventually electronic tagging will be introduced.

Movement Forms

You must complete AML (Animal Movement License) forms for taking animals both to the show and bringing them back again. These can be obtained from your Local Authority Animal Health Divisional Office and must be returned to them on completion. You are required to keep your copies for 3 years, so a good filing system will help. You must keep a flock register to record movements both on and off your holding.

As Defra is continually evolving its animal identification policy you should receive regular updates as a registered keeper of sheep, but errors do occur, so periodically check the Defra website for the latest industry news.

Protection & Surveillance Zones

These are used to control the movement of animals where cases of certain diseases are known to be present. At the time of writing this book Blue Tongue is being controlled in this way and has some important ramifications for breeders wishing to attend shows.

Generally speaking you cannot move your stock out of these zones unless they have been protected from vector attack by vaccination. As you probably realise, this immediately causes a problem if you want to show at the Royal for instance and you don't fall in the same zone as will be the case with many exhibitors wishing to attend this prestigious event.

Vaccination for breeders wishing to show outside their zones is a must, but unfortunately this isn't the end of it. Movement can only take place by complying with the requirements of either the EXD482(BT) or the EXD483(BT) license. This involves disinfecting vehicles and animals with a Defra approved insecticide, undergoing veterinary tests, signing self-declaration certificates plus various other conditions which are too detailed to be listed here. The licenses are easily obtainable from Defra and can be downloaded from its website.

If by now you are thinking that all this is far too much trouble, don't despair. You should be able to find some shows within your own zone where movements will be easier, or hopefully the disease will be fully controlled and the zones will no longer be necessary. If that is the case it does no harm to be aware of what procedures may be put into place should similar outbreaks occur.

Maedi Visna (MV)

This disease isn't very common, but it is said to be on the increase and is taken very seriously by commercial flock breeders and producers of terminal sires such as Suffolk, Texel, Beltex etc.

It is caused by a slow virus infection that produces an increase in the numbers of adult sheep in poor condition, resulting in a higher proportion of barren ewes and smaller lambs.

Other signs include pneumonia, mastitis, arthritis and hind limb paralysis. It isn't easy to diagnose as the symptoms are similar to other diseases and matters are not helped by most vets never having seen a case. There is no cure, no vaccine and the outcome is inevitably fatal.

The best option is to avoid contracting the disease in the first place which is the purpose of the Maedi Visna Accreditation scheme. This is a voluntary scheme run by the Scottish Agricultural College and involves blood tests on sheep over 12 months of age and then two yearly tests thereafter. If proved to be free of the disease your flock will receive MV Accreditation.

Showing Sheep

This is important to breeders of commercial sheep and terminal sire producers as many shows will only accept MV Accredited entries and it can give an edge when it comes to selling stock in the autumn sales. However, it isn't compulsory to join the scheme and many sheep keepers are not members. Owners of rare and native breeds in particular are not usually members of the scheme. Smaller shows will isolate Accredited and Non-Accredited animals into their own rings, separated by a corridor several feet wide. The judge will examine each lot separately and then wash his hands before giving the other ring the once over.

You will be required to say whether you are a member of the MV scheme and if so, will usually be asked to submit a photocopy of your certificate as proof.

Scrapie

This is a fatal brain disease of sheep and sometimes goats. How it is contracted and spread isn't really known. Symptoms develop gradually over months or years, the typical ones being scratching, trembling, excitability, hind limb weakness and loss of condition. There is no cure and no treatment. This is a notifiable disease so suspicions must be reported.

In 2001 the National Scrapie Plan was implemented to try to breed sheep naturally resistant to Scrapie. Many pedigree breeders have taken part in the Ram Genotyping Scheme which, after testing, gives stock rams a score relating to their Scrapie resistance. This will be used to good advantage when it comes to selling breeding stock.

Certificate of Health

If you are resident outside the UK you will need a Certificate of Health and the appropriate return certificate to enable you to return to your own country. Your local Animal Health Divisional Office will be able to help with this.

Transport License

If you expect to travel over 40 miles (about 65km), you will need to obtain a certificate of competence to show that you can safely transport animals from one destination to another. This new EU regulation aims to ensure high minimum standards of welfare for all animals whilst they are being transported to and from markets, slaughter and on export journeys in both the UK and throughout the European Union.

There are two types of certificate tests:

Short Journey - for trips over 40 miles (65km) and for up to eight hours

Long Journey - for trips over 40 miles (65km) and over eight hours.

You only need to take the test once. Various bodies such as the National Farmers Union and local colleges offer the tests which vary in price.

Chapter Twelve
Other Types of Shows

So far this book has covered mainly summer agricultural and breed society shows as the principle opportunities for showing off your stock. For most people these will certainly form the thrust of the showing season, but there are other types of competitions, depending on breed, in which you may be interested in taking part.

Fleece Competitions

Due to some pretty active promotion by the British Wool Marketing Board fleece competitions are becoming more and more popular with many shepherds who prefer to show the fleece rather than the animal itself.

You will find fleece classes at most of the major agricultural shows which have often been sponsored by the British Wool Marketing Board who also supply expert judges. The rules are simple and entry fees low at about £3 per entry, but you may find that you have to be a registered wool producer to enter.

This can be done through the British Wool Marketing Board website or by contacting them via post. There is no cost but you do need a minimum of six sheep to become a producer.

Like every other aspect of showing, to stand a chance of winning with a fleece you need to prepare in much the same way as if showing "on the hoof." Never having shown in fleece classes myself, the advice here has been gleaned from those who have, but do check with your particular breed society for any variations.

Sort Early

The initial step comes months before the first show by ensuring that any likely animals are fed well and maintain good health. Illness and poor condition scoring reflects in the fleece, so these aspects should not be overlooked. As each breed has different fibre characteristics it isn't possible to list here what you should be looking for. This will be covered by the breed standard. Experts maintain that they are looking for sheep that will shear well and have often found that shearlings produce the best fleeces.

About 4-5 weeks before shearing, wash the fleece. For best results select a good drying day as wet wool attracts even more dirt than when dry. When shearing, be extra careful to get the fleece off in one piece. If you are not doing it yourself point out to the shearer that the fleece is intended for showing so you don't want blood spots from any nicks scattered amongst the wool. Similarly, try to avoid the use of markers and sprays.

Straw, bracken and soiled wool should also be removed. When the fleece is as clean and tidy as possible, carefully wrap it in the correct manner as advised by the British Wool Marketing Board.

Showing Sheep

Fleece Presentation

Find a clean area and throw out the fleece, flesh side down. Fleeces from the Blackface, Herdwick and Rough Fell breeds should be laid flesh side up. Pick off any extraneous matter and remove any daggings which may have been missed pre-shearing.

Include only clean, dry belly wool with the fleece before folding in the flanks toward the centre. Turn in the britch end and roll the fleece firmly and neatly towards the neck. After rolling, part the fleece. Without twisting, tuck the neck wool firmly into the body of the fleece. The fleece should now be firm and secure. Store in a clean sack or bag.

Carcase Competitions

It's easy to forget that the ultimate purpose of breeding sheep is to produce quality meat that will find a ready market. Carcase competitions, though not everyone's cup of tea, are actually a good form of promotion, especially if you are selling at the farm gate as the kudos of adding an award winning rosette to your advertising material can only be of benefit.

Many agricultural shows put on classes often sponsored by a local food processor. The show society will buy lambs from the producer at the going market rate and have them slaughtered. The prepared carcase is kept refrigerated throughout the competition. Marks are awarded for: hind quarter, fore quarter, fat cover, colour and texture.

Other Types of Shows

Entry fees are charged and prize money is awarded to the winners.

Usually you will be able to show a single lamb, either under 20kg or over 20kg. Some shows, however, may insist on more. The rules are very straight forward and will be explained fully in the show schedules.

Sales

Sheep sales tend to take place at the end of the summer and throughout the autumn. This is when people look for new stock, move surplus stock and buy in rams either as terminal sires or to improve an existing pedigree flock.

Breed societies hold sales and so do most livestock markets, all of which may be preceded by show classes. In the case of livestock markets, the animals may or may not be judged in a ring, but usually not if only one or two prizes are offered. In this case, selections are made from the pens. At the big sales where proper show classes are being staged these are often held on one day with the sale itself taking place the next. One of the biggest show and sale events is the Traditional & Native Breeds Show and Sale held in September, currently at Melton Mowbray Market.

Sheep entered into shows/sales are obviously destined to fall under the auctioneer's hammer, so the desire to win a prize becomes even more important as this will affect the selling price. Breeders tend to trim their best animals, especially for their society sales, but lesser quality stock that hasn't been entered into the show section of the sale or is not expected to be a prize winner is usually left untrimmed or just has the backs done.

Appendices

Breed Standards and Descriptions

Have you ever wondered exactly how a judge arrives at his decision? Contrary to what some breeders think he isn't simply picking his best friend's favourite! He is looking for examples of a breed's typical characteristics as laid down by its breed standard or description.

All pure bred animals which have a society to promote them have a set of standards or a detailed description to help breeders produce the ideal specimen. If you keep pedigree sheep a copy of your breed standard or description is a must. Different societies present them in different ways, but all will be broken down into various body parts describing what is ideal and in some cases what is not!

Some characteristics will be common to all breeds; general conformation is something all sheep breeders aim for, but as any sheep breeder knows, there are wide variations in other areas which a pedigree breeder needs to be aware of.

When a judge is examining an exhibit he will be keeping these descriptions in mind and assessing how a particular sheep measures up against the ideal. As some standards list faults which are so bad that they merit disqualification he will also be checking for these; yet another reason why pedigree breeders must be very familiar with their breed's characteristics.

With over forty different breeds of sheep in existence it isn't possible to list all the standards or descriptions for each breed, but here are a few to give you an idea of what judges base their decisions on.

Commercial Breeds

These breeds provide most of the lamb on our tables. They have detailed pedigrees and are used to provide terminal sires which are crossed with specially bred hybrids such as the Masham. They can also be run as pure-bred commercial flocks as they have good lambing averages and rapid growth rates. Top quality stock can fetch many hundreds or even thousands of pounds. The downside is they need intensive feeding of expensive concentrates to maximise their potential.

Suffolk

General - Rams should be masculine, muscular, good sized and well proportioned. Ewes should be feminine and smooth, with a softer look. Both rams and ewes should be structurally and reproductively sound and aesthetically attractive.

Head - Should be black, hornless, free of wrinkles, and well covered with a thick, fine hair. The muzzle needs to be long, smooth and roman with a deep jaw that presents incisor teeth that meet the pad. Ears should be long and bell shaped, angling down towards the corner of the mouth. Eyes should be bright, full and well set.

Neck - Of moderate length. Shoulders should show volume, but blending and sloping smoothly from neck into barrel. This smooth flow of contour helps with ease of lambing.

Chest & Lower Rib - Should be wide and deep. These dimensions should be carried back into the lower rib. Ewes should exhibit capacity and rib to convert forages and carry multiple lambs.

Back & Loin - The back should have a straight spine from the base of the neck to the tail head. The ribs should be wide and well sprung at top, carrying down deep. The loin should be wide, long and thick in depth.

Rump - Should be long, wide and level from hooks to pins. Ideally, the width of the sheep across the hooks should be equal to one third of its height at the withers. The tail head should be wide and level and well set, carrying width down through stifles. It should be enhanced with a broad, deep, full twist. This area is the heaviest meat producing area of the carcase.

Legs and Feet - The legs should be straight and black with good, heavy, flat, smooth bones in the shanks. Fore and rear legs set well apart. Front legs should be set under the animal and not out at sides. Pasterns should be short with toes pointing straight ahead. An animal should walk with a long, smooth gait and should track as wide or wider on the hind legs as the front legs. These points accommodate a heavy, fast growing body with structural soundness and mobility and contribute to the attractiveness of the animal.

Fleece, Skin and Belly - The fleece should be dense, free of dark fibre and not shading into dark hair or wool. Belly should be well covered with wool. Wool should not extend below the knees and hocks. Skin should be soft and pink.

Reproductive Areas - The testicles on rams should be of even, smooth symmetrical shape with the epididymids well defined. They are contained by a scrotum that is not split at the bottom. Ewes that are milking should have well developed udders (like a very large half of cantaloupe melon) with teats of medium length and circumference, which are well placed. Vulvas on ewes should be of good shape and point down. Ewes should exhibit large capacity, especially through the reproductive areas to facilitate and carry multiple lambs.

Texel

General - Meat conformation is the most desirable characteristic and should normally be apparent. A roomy well-structured body is desirable together with blocky conformation. A mature ram should weigh about 80 kg and a mature ewe about 60 kg.

Head - Crown to nose should be wide. Eyes bright and clear, nostrils well spread, dark, preferably black. Mouth broad. Poll flat with no wool. Ears well set, ideally "Ten to Two."

Forequarters - Neck well muscled, but not too short. Shoulders flat on top and no wider than the rib cage which should be deep with the sheep appearing wedge shaped. Characteristics to be avoided are neck too long, narrow or shallow forequarters and hollow behind the shoulders.

Body - Strong and powerful, well muscled from front to back. Back and loins sufficiently long and broad with ribs deep and well sprung. Loins as wide and deep as possible. Avoid an uneven top line, ribs too flat or too shallow and a narrow or angular loin.

Quarters & Gigots - Area between top of haunch bone tail as long and wide as proportionately possible. Curved, fully rounded hips. Well developed gigots. Tail short, narrow and woolly. Avoid too narrow hips or gigots and straight or poorly muscled gigots.

Legs - Should be proportionate to the body. The sheep should stand square and straight. Back legs well sprung from the hock. Rams should stand well up on short pasterns. Wooled to middle of forearm and hind to middle of shank. Remainder of legs covered in fine hair. Feet deep, hard and black. Avoid front legs too narrowly set or too wide apart and overly straight or curved hind legs.

Fleece - Dense and tightly stapled. Well crimped and lustrous. Avoid kemp, bare neck, belly or tail and loose staples. The staple is the name given to naturally occurring clusters or locks of wool fibres that are held together by cross fibres which form the fleece. All sheep wool is made up of staples, but due to the extra length of the longwools they can become very knotted and need separating before showing.

Colour – White fleece, face and legs.

Charollais

General – This is a terminal sire so emphasis on selection should be placed on its excellent fleshing qualities and growth. The purpose of the breed is to breed rams for crossing with commercial ewes to produce quality meat lambs for slaughter. Easy lambing is an important trait associated with the breed so skeletal structure to ensure this is essential. The fineness of bone of the breed also contributes to the higher killing out percentage of their progeny.

Shoulders and Topline - Shoulders should be well fleshed and level. They should not be narrow and pointed, nor too heavy and coarse. The breed should not carry excessive fat over the shoulder. Topline should be strong and level with good length.

Head - A good Charollais head is full of character, alert without wool. The skin colour is pink with a varying amount of creamy, sandy or white coloured hair. The varying amount of hair gives animals within the breed a difference in appearance. A distinctive feature of the breed is a white flash above each eye. Regional / breeder preferences as to amount and colour of head hair are acceptable. Heads should not be too small in the muzzle and should be broad between the eyes. Females should have a kind head and rams a stronger masculine head. Heads should not be too wide as Charollais rams are renowned for their easy lambing.

Teeth - should ideally be short, straight and directly onto the pad. Deviations away from this optimum either back, forward or splayed are undesirable.

Feet and Pasterns - Feet should be neat and balanced, cleats should not be open nor mis-shapen. Pasterns should be short, straight and upright.

Front Legs - Straight, balanced legs are most desirable; neither too close nor too wide apart. They should be a good colour. Bone should neither be too fine or heavy. Soundness of movement is important.

Back Legs - Should be set well apart but not extreme. There should be good definition of hock, not over bent or too straight. Bone should neither be too fine or heavy. Good balanced mobility is important.

Testicles - Rams must have two adequately sized testicles of approximately the same size and normal consistency.

Udder - Ewes should have no hardness, lumps or malformation in the udder.

Loin - Should be long, wide and deep. The eye muscle should be full. Animals should not be over fat across the loin.

Gigot - The gigot should be thick, deep and full. The rump should be thick and wide. Narrow, sloping rumps are undesirable.

Growth - Growth is important in the breed, therefore well grown sheep are of merit. However sheep which are just tall and without good fleshing qualities are not of merit. Big is only beautiful if accompanied with good loin and gigot.

Fleece - The breed should have a good quality fleece, dense but not too long nor open. It should be complete over the body without breaks but not extending down the legs or over the head.

Beltex

General - Primarily a terminal sire to cross with British sheep and half-bred continental sheep. The breed's main characteristics are double-muscled hindquarters coupled with fine bones.

Head – Broad and covered in close white fur. Eyes dark. Ears short and forward facing.

Fleece – white and close.

Legs – white and covered in short fur. Should stand square.

Body – Double muscling of the hindquarters.

Border Leicester

General - The Border Leicester is a direct descendant of the Dishley Leicesters, bred and made famous by the great livestock breeding pioneer, Robert Bakewell of Dishley Grange, Leicestershire. A distinctive sheep, it is large with a proud and graceful stance. The long, upright ears give it a unique appearance.

Body - Long back, level and well fleshed. Well sprung in ribs with well-developed chest and gigot and level underline. Will be well fleshed and firm underhand. Rams will stand about 80-85 cm at the shoulder, measure 100cm from crown to tail.

Fleece – White wool of even quality, densely planted with a good staple length that should cover the whole body.

Head - Should be thoroughly masculine, (in rams, softer in ewes), have a well developed muzzle with wide black nostrils. Eyes should be clear, bold and dark, ears a good length, carried at an alert angle and covered with hair, the crown smooth and clear of wool. The teeth should be regular and meet the pad.

Neck - Tapering nicely from the head, should be strongly set at the shoulders.

Legs - Well filled gigots should be carried on legs squarely set under the body, strong with clean flat bones, covered with white hair and free of wool. The feet sound and dark in colour.

Native Breeds

With spiralling food and transport costs cutting profit margins to even thinner proportions, interest in our native breeds has increased quite rapidly in recent years. The fact that they have evolved to adapt to local climate and geographical conditions means they will thrive and finish on poorer pasture and need less in the way of concentrates than their more rapidly growing continental cousins. The following are some of the most popular.

Jacob

General - An alert, active sheep being upstanding and deep bodied. Both sexes are horned. Ewes should be of a fine feminine appearance and rams thicker set and masculine. They are hardy with good mothering abilities. Single and twins are usual, but triplets and quads are not uncommon.

Head – No wool forward of horns. Clear white blaze desirable with even black cheeks. Dark nose preferred. Adult sheep with pink noses in conjunction with broad white face are undesirable. Dark, bold eyes with no tendency to split eye-lid deformity.

Horns - Number two or four. Where there are four the top pair should grow upward from the top of the head and have no forward growing tendencies. There should preferably be space between the top and lower horns. Where there are just two horns there should preferably be space between the roots of the horns at the crown of the head, and grow so as to leave space between horn and cheek. Black horns are preferred. They should at all times give the animal freedom from injury and comfort when feeding.

Neck - Strong, of medium length, well set on shoulder.

Body – The back should be straight, level from base of neck to setting on the tail, which should be broad. Well sprung ribs, body well let down, forming a good bottom line. Tail to be well set up on chine with well developed thigh.

Legs - Medium boned of medium length, clear of wool below knee and hock. Preferably white with little or no black.

Fleece - Of a medium quality, white with well defined black patches. It is preferred that skin beneath the white wool be a good pink, and black beneath the dark wool. There should be little or no kemp. Mottled wool and skin is undesirable.

Kerry Hill

General - The breed dates back to 1809 and comes from the village of Kerry in the Welsh Borders. It has been bred to survive in harsh conditions, with good foraging abilities. The rams are ideal to use on Hill and Longwool breeds to produce large, lean lambs.

The ewes are good mothers and milk well even on poor grazing. They are long-lived and can easily achieve a lambing percentage of 175% with the lambs growing well and maturing early. They can be marketed at 16kg at 12 – 14 weeks, or if kept on as stores will produce a lean carcase of 20 – 25kg the following spring.

Head - White face with sharply defined black markings on the nose, eyes, ears and legs. The ears are small and upright and should be free of wool. Both sexes are polled, with mature rams weighing on average 65 – 70kg and ewes 55 – 60kg.

Fleece - White and dense. It is one of the softest British wool types used for tweeds, flannel, knitwear and furnishing fabrics.

Romney

General – Originally from the low lying areas of Kent and Sussex adjoining the English Channel. They are hardy and docile and do not stray far from their territory. Sometimes known as Kent sheep they became so popular that they spread all over the world. Noted for their wool, which is produced from heavy, long-wooled fleeces weighing from 4-5kg.

Head – Wide and level between the ears. No horns or dark hair on the poll. Eyes should be large, bright and prominent. Mouth full and sound. Faces in ewes full, rams broad and masculine in appearance. Should be white and skin of a clean pink colour. Noses and hooves should be black.

Body – Neck well set into shoulders, strong and not too long. Shoulders well put in and level with the back which should be straight and long with a wide and deep loin. Chest wide and deep. Rump wide, deep and well turned. Tail set in, almost level with chine. Thighs well let down and developed. Ribs well sprung.

Legs - Well set and of good bone and sound feet. Sheep should stand well on their pasterns.

Fleece - Should be white in colour, of even texture and of a good decided staple from top of the head to end of tail and free of kemp.

Shetland

General – Shetlands are the smallest of the native breeds and originate from the Shetland Isles. They are small built animals with a distinctive head, often carrying wool on the forehead. Eyes should be bright, ears small and erect.

Legs – Should be fine and of medium length.

Tail – quite distinctive, being broad at the base and tapering to the point.

Horns - Rams have round horns, but ewes are naturally polled.

Wool – Should be very fine with a soft, silky feel. The fleece usually weighs 1 - 1.5kg when reared on hill ground, but can increase in weight on better pasture. Staple length is approximately 10cm, with a wavy, tight crimp.

Colour - mainly white, but various other shades can occur. Reddish brown, (moorit), steel grey, (shaela) and black, which is really dark brown. Variations of these shades can arise, but they are less common.

Hebridean

General - As their name suggests these sheep originate from the outer Scottish Isles and are sometimes known as St. Kilda sheep. They are small, fine boned sheep with black wool and two or more horns. Ewes weigh about 40kg with rams proportionately larger.

Legs - Long and thin and delicate below the hocks. The feet are small with exceptionally hard horn.

Showing Sheep

Body - The body is relatively long for an animal of the size with well sprung ribs. The back should be level throughout. It is not inclined to fatness or to carrying excess condition. Mature adults even on good keep rarely have a body condition score greater than 3.

Fleece - Dense and weather-proof with true black being the most desirable colour. Some sheep go grey with age. No other colouration, spots or patches should be present in animals of more than a few weeks of age. Selected fleece is very sought after by hand spinners and weavers.

Mothering - Mature ewes normally produce twins, even under less than ideal conditions. They are excellent mothers and lamb very easily, even when crossbred with meat sires, and produce relatively large amounts of milk.

Adaptability – Able to adapt successfully to a wide range of managements. Often used as part of parkland management on large estates in England and Scotland. Their dietary preferences differ from those of other breeds and this, together with their ability to thrive on vegetation with poor energy values, makes them a unique environmental management tool.

Rare Breeds

The Rare Breeds Survival Trusts monitors Britain's sheep breeds and when numbers fall below certain levels they are added to the Trust's Watch List. The following are amongst those currently causing concern:

Appendices - Breed Standards

Soay

General - If you have wondered what British sheep were like before Viking and Roman invaders introduced their own stock, look no further than the Soay. These small framed, late maturing, brown fleeced sheep originate from the island of Soay in the St. Kilda group of islands off the coast of Scotland and were extremely numerous before the Roman occupation.

They are excellent conservation grazers, happy in woodland and on hillsides. The coloured fleece is sought after for many craft uses and their carcase produces lean meat of a delicious flavour which is much favoured by the gourmet trade.

They are also a favourite of both parks and country estates which is why they are often seen many miles from their native wind swept islands.

A peculiarity of the breed is the lack of flocking instinct. Try to work them with a dog at your peril! The result is usually a scattered stampede with many hours of tedious work locating individual flock members!

Horns – Rams have two strong horns. Ewes are either two-horned, polled, or scurred.

Fleece - Can vary from soft, fine wool to more coarse hairy fibres known as "kemps" and mixtures in-between. Colour is mainly brown but white, beige and other variations often occur. The fleece is normally shed naturally.

Tail – Short and thin.

Withers – Prominent.

Showing Sheep

Manx Loaghtan

General - The Manx Loaghtan comes from the Isle of Man. It is similar to the Hebridean, which leads some breeders to think it is descended from Viking stock. Others disagree, arguing that there is little evidence of this.

The word Loaghtan comes from lugh dhoan which means mouse-brown. This has now become the established colour in the Isle of Man, although they were formerly also seen in white and black.

Head – Fine and covered in dark brown fur. Sometimes carries a top knot of wool.

Legs – Free from wool and dark brown.

Horns – Both sexes carry horns, either two or preferably four which curve in a backwards sweep. Sometimes six horns are present. Horns on rams are bigger and stronger.

Carcase - They produce a lean, low cholesterol carcase weighing up to 18kg with the meat being of high quality and flavour. Like most primitives they are slow maturing and are normally killed at around 15 months of age.

Fleece – Some animals may shed their wool naturally, others need to be sheared. Loaghtan wool is normally left undyed and used to weave lightweight garments. Manx tartans are also made from this wool. Stockings, once made from the wool of the Loaghtan were much prized by the islanders. The breed is free of Wool Marketing Board restrictions, which means it can be sold direct to hand spinners.

Ryeland

General - Although the breed specification speaks of Ryelands being white, they are available as coloured animals with many breeders keeping both. Blacks, browns and varying shades of grey are common, but all pedigree animals must be white throughout.

Head - Should be medium in length, masculine in rams, with no trace of horn. The face should show character, strength and constitution and should be a dull white in colour with dark skin around the nose and nostrils not contracted. White hair on dark skin around the eye, with eye bright and clear of wool.

Ears - Medium length, carried slightly back, dark colour with either fine white hair or short white wool. The neck should be strong, broad and set so as to give the head a bridled appearance.

Shoulders - Well set, no depression behind.

Chest - Broad and fairly deep with a good, straight back, level from base of neck to setting of tail, which should be broad.

Body - Well sprung rib cage and body well down to form a good bottom line. The legs of mutton should also be full and well let down with good length of hind quarter from hip bone to dock.

Legs - Should be dull white in colour, legs below knee and hock all straight with compact feet firmly set. Feet also dull white.

Fleece - Needs to be good in quality, stronger in rams than in ewes, deep in staple, thickly set on skin, handling firmly, close, level appearance, every part including belly and purse well covered, except where otherwise stated. No coarseness, kemp, black, grey or rusty fibres.

Flesh - should be even and firm to handle and the skin a healthy pink colour.

Portland

General - The Portland is a heathland breed originating from the Isle of Portland, just off the Dorset coast. The breed produces exceptionally high quality meat with fine texture and excellent flavour. It can lamb at any time of year but usually produces a single lamb which is born with a foxy red coat which changes in the first few months to a creamy white.

Body - The body is of a primitive type within the Downs breeds, with good width between the legs. The tail is long and set well up on the rump. A typical ewe weighs 38-40kg.

Legs - Fine boned with an even tan colour. The front legs and hind legs below the hock should be free from wool. The hooves should be uniformly dark, small and straight.

Head – The face is a tan colour, but may have lighter areas around the eyes and muzzle. The nose is dark. Some sheep carry a light covering of wool on the forehead, but the rest of the face is free from wool.

Horns - Light coloured. Rams are heavily spiralled. Ewes curve through a half circle. There is often a black line in one or both horns.

Fleece - Close and fine with a short staple, though some red kemp fibres may be found on the britch.

North Ronaldsay

General - Primitive northern short-tailed sheep representing a very early stage in the evolution of domestic sheep. DNA studies have shown a close relationship to sheep found in the Stone Age village of Skara Brae on mainland Orkney.

In 1832 a wall was built around their native island to confine the animals to the foreshore for most of the year in order to conserve the inland grazing. Since then the breed has developed its distinctive metabolism due to its diet of seaweed, which also renders it susceptible to copper poisoning under standard sheep management systems. Animals need to be at least 15 months old to reach marketable weight, but the meat is lean and full of flavour.

Body - Small and fine-boned. Rams often have a heavy mane and beard. Adult ewes weigh around 25kg and are excellent mothers, giving birth to small, lively lambs.

Head – Face is slightly dished and rams heavily horned. Ewes can also be horned, scurred or polled.

Fleece - The double fleece has coarse outer guard hairs and a fine soft inner coat. The wool is suitable for handicraft work and knitting yarn and is popular with hand spinners. It also felts well and has good handicraft potential. Colours include white, various shades of grey, black and moorit (deep brown).

Showing Sheep

Health and Movement

DEFRA
Customer Contact Unit, Eastbury House, 30-34 Albert Embankment, London, SE1 7TL Tel: 08459 33 55 77
helpline@defra.gsi.gov.uk, www.defra.gov.uk

DARD
Department of Agricultural & Rural Development, Dundonald House, Upper Newtownards Road, Belfast, BT4 3SB Tel: 028 9052 4420

Scottish Government Agriculture Tel: 0131 556 8400
08457 741741 (UK local rate) ceu@scotland.gsi.gov.uk
www.scotland.gov.uk/topics/agriculture

Welsh Government Agriculture, Department for Rural Affairs, Welsh Assembly Government, Cathays Park, Cardiff, CF10 3NQ Tel: 0845 010 3300, rah.
requests@wales.gsi.gov.uk,www.new.wales.gov.uk

British Wool Marketing Board, Wool House, Roydsdale Way, Euroway Trading Estate, Bradford, BD4 6SE
Tel: 01274 688666, mail@britishwool.org.uk
www.britishwool.org.uk

Maedi-Visna Accreditation Scheme (run by the Scottish Agricultural College) Scottish Agricultural College, Work King's Buildings, West Mains Road, Edinburgh, EH9 3JG Tel: 0131 535 4000
www.sac.ac.uk

National Scrapie Plan Administration Centre, Whittington Road, Worcester, WR5 2SU Tel: 0845 601 4858 nspac@animalhealth.gsi.gov.uk

Animal Ultrasound Scanning Ltd., Crawshaw Farm, Bradfield, Sheffield, S6 6HU Tel: 0114 285 1315 www.crawshawfarm.co.uk

Animal Housing

Robinsons (Scotland) Ltd., Broomhouses, 2 Ind. Est., Old Glasgow Rd., Lockerbie, DG11 2SD Tel: 01576 205905 www.rbscotland.co.uk

Farmplus Constructions Ltd., Shay Lane, Longridge, Lancashire, PR3 3BT Tel: 01772 785252 www.farmplus.co.uk

Show Supplies and Equipment

The Halter Lady, 2 Chartwood, Loggerheads, Market Drayton, Shropshire, TF9 4RJ Tel: 01630 672368 mrshampshire@thehalterlady.co.uk www.thehalterlady.co.uk

Peasridges Sheep Services Ltd. (Grooming Equipment) Stonelink, Stubb Lane, Brede, Nr. Rye, E. Sussex, TN31 6BL Tel: 01424 882900, www.peasridge.co.uk

Modulamb (Sheep Handling Equipment), Peter Hall Farm, Coombefields, Coventry, CV2 2DR Tel: 02476 611647 www.modulamb.com

Showing Sheep

Burgon & Ball (Hand Shears) La Plata Works, Holme Lane, Sheffield, S6 4JY Tel: 0114 233 8262, www.burgonandball.com

Llugwy Farm (Show Coats,) Llanbister Road, Powys, LD1 5UT Tel: 01547 550641 www.llugwy-farm.co.uk

Showtime Supplies, Pear tree Farm, Fangfoss, York, YO41 5QH Tel: 01759 368588 www.showtime-supplies.co.uk

Shearwell Data Ltd. (Ear tags),Putham Farm, Wheddon Cross, Minehead, Somerset, TA24 7AS Tel: 01643 841611 www.shearwell.co.uk

Sheep Societies

National Sheep Association
The Sheep Centre, Malvern, Worcestershire, WR13 6PH Tel:01684 892 661 www.nationalsheep.org.uk

Beulah Speckled Face Sheep Society
Dennis J. Jones (Society Secretary), The Firs, 63 Garth Road, Builth Wells, Powys, LD2 3NH Tel: 01982 553726 www.beulahsheep.co.uk

The Blackface Sheep Breeders Association
Aileen McFadzean *(Promotions Manager)*, Woodhead of Mailer, Perth, PH2 0QA ¡Tel/Fax: 01738 634018 www.scottish-blackface.co.uk

Appendices - Sheep Societies

Black Welsh Mountain Sheep Breeders Association
Lake Villa, Bradworthy, Holsworthy, Devon, EX22 7SQ
Tel: 01409 241579 www.blackwelshmountain.org.uk

Bluefaced Leicester Sheep Breeders Association
Jean Gibbon *(Breed Secretary),* Furmiston, Carsphairn,
Castle Douglas, DG7 3TE Tel: 01644 460647
www.blueleicester.co.uk

The Society of Border Leicester Sheep Breeders
Ian J. R. Sutherland *(Secretary),* Rock Midstead, Alnwick,
Northumberland, NE66 2TH Tel: 01665 579326,
www.borderleicesters.co.uk

Cheviot Sheep Society
Isobel McVittie (Secretary), Holm Cottage, Langholm,
Dumfriesshire, DG13 0JP Tel: 01387 380222
www.cheviotsheep.org

Clun Forest Sheep Breeders Society
Ms. Davina Stanhope *(Secretary),* 2 Upper Longwood,
Eaton Constantine, Shrewsbury, Shropshire, SY5 6SB
Tel: 01952 740731 www.clunforestsheep.co.uk

Dalesbred Sheep Breeders Association
Mr J Whitaker *(Secretary),* Gib Hey Cottage, Chipping,
Nr. Preston, Lancashire, PR3 2WU Tel: 01995 61570

Dartmoor Sheep Breeders Association
info@greyface-dartmoor.org.uk
www.greyface-dartmoor.org.uk

Derbyshire Gritstone Sheep Breed Society
Mrs. S. Coppack, 5 Bridge Close, Waterfoot, Rossendale,
Lancashire, BB4 9SN Tel: 01706 228520

Showing Sheep

Devon Closewool Sheep Breeders Association
Ron Smith, 1 Rectory Close, Filleigh, Barnstaple,
EX32 0SD Tel: 01598 760359
ron@holtomandthomas.co.uk,
www.devonclosewool.co.uk

Devon and Cornwall Longwool Flock Book Association
Mr. M. Britton *(Secretary)*, Peckham View, Kentisbeare,
Cullompton, Devon, EX15 2EY Tel: 01884 266201

The Dorset Down Sheep Breeders' Association
Carolyn Opie, Havett Farm, Dobwalls, Liskeard, Cornwall,
PL14 6HB Tel: 01579 320273
secretary@dorsetdownsheep.org.uk, www.
dorsetdownsheep.org.uk

Dorset Horn and Poll Dorset Sheep Breeder's Association
Agriculture House, Acland Road, Dorchester, Dorset,
DT1 1EF Tel: 01305 262126 mail@dorsetsheep.org
www.dorsetsheep.org

Exmoor Horn Sheep Breeders' Society
Mrs Gina Rawle, Kitridge Farm, Withypool, Somerset,
TA24 7RY Tel: 01643 831593
info@exmoorhornbreeders.co.uk
www.exmoorhornbreeders.co.uk

Hampshire Down Sheep Breeders' Association
Richard Davis *(Secretary)*, Rickyard Cottage, Denner Hill,
Great Missenden, Buckinghamshire, HP16 0HZ
Tel: 01494 488388 richard@rickyard.plus.com
www.hampshiredownsociety.org.uk

Appendices - Sheep Societies

Herdwick Sheep Breeders' Association
The Old Stables, Redhills, Penrith, Cumbria, CA11 0DT
Tel: 01768 869533 info@herdwick-sheep.com
www.herdwick-sheep.com

The Jacob Sheep Society
Louise Smith, Oaktree Farm, Buttermilk Lane, Yarningale
Common, Claverdon, Warks., CV35 8HP, 01926 843434
secretary@jacobsheep.org.uk,
www.jacobsheep.freeserve.co.uk

Kerry Hill Flock Book Society
The Bramleys, Broadheath, Presteigne, Powys, LD8 2HG
Tel: 01544 267353 www.kerryhill.net

Leicester Longwool Sheep Breeders' Assocation
Barry Enderby *(Secretary)*, Coppelade, Wallisgate,
Whaplode, Spalding, Lincs., PE12 6UB Tel: 01406 424242
www.leicesterlongwoolsheepassociation.co.uk

Lincoln Longwool Sheep Breeders' Association
Ruth Mawer *(Secretary)*, Lincolnshire Showground.
Grange de Lings, Lincoln, LN2 2NA Tel: 01522 56866
lincolnlongwool@lineone.net

LLanwenog Sheep Society
M. Green , **Tel:** 01570 423 135
llanwenogsheep@hotmail.com
www.llanwenog-sheep.co.uk

Lleyn Sheep Society
Gwenda Roberts *(Soc. Secretary)*, Gwyndy, Bryncroes Sarn,
Pwllheli, Gwynedd, LL53 8ET Tel: 01758 730366
office@lleynsheep.com www.lleynsheep.com

Showing Sheep

Lonk Sheep Breeders' Association
Mrs. J. Shorrock *(Secretary)*, 51 Glen View Road,
Burnley, Lancashire, BB11 2QW Tel: 01282 433047
www.york.ac.uk/org/cnap/tst/breeds/lonk

Masham Sheep Breeders' Association
Val Lawson *(Secretary)*, Oakbank, Bentham, Lancaster,
Lancashire, LA2 7DW Tel: 01524 261606

North Country Cheviot Sheep Breeders' Society
Alison Brodie *(Secretary)*, Wallacehall, West Waterbeck,
Lockerbie. E-mail: info@nc-cheviot.co.uk
www.nc-cheviot. co.uk

Oxford Down Sheep Breeders' Association
John S. Brigg, Bishop's Gorse, Lighthorne, Warwick,
CV35 0BB Tel: 01926 651273
john@oxforddownsheep.org.uk
www.oxforddown.members.beeb.net

Hill Radnor Flock Book Society
Mr. John Lewis, 16 Ship Street, Brecon, Powys,
LD3 9AD Tel: 01874 623200 jal@montague-harris.co.uk
www.hill-radnor.co.uk

Romney Sheep Breeders' Society
Alan West, 2 Woodland Close, West Malling, Kent,
ME19 6RR Tel: 01732 845637 alan.t.west@internet.com

Rough Fell Sheep Breeders' Association
Amanda Croft, High Newstead Farm, Jervaulx, Masham,
Ripon, North Yorkshire, HG4 4PJ Tel: 01677 460241
roughfell@fsmail.net
www.roughfellsheep.co.uk

Ryeland Flock Book Society

Holly Cottage, Playley Green, Redmarley, Glos., GL19 3NB
www.ryelandfbs.com

Shetland Sheep Society

Jean Bennett *(Secretary)*, Shielhope, Chatton, Alnwick,
Northumberland, NE66 5RE ben_hen2@yahoo.co.uk
www.users.zetnet.co.uk

Shropshire Sheep Breeders' Association

Jane Wilson (Secretary) Tel: 01434 240435
shropshire_sheep@hotmail.com
www.shropshire-sheep.co.uk

Suffolk Sheep Society

The Sheep Centre, Malvern, Worcs., WR13 6PH
Tel: 01684 893366 enquiries@suffolksheep.org
www.suffolksheep.org

Swaledale Sheep Breeders' Association

Alan Alderson, Barras Farm, Barras, Kirkby Stephen,
Cumbria, CA17 4ET Tel: 017683 41397
alanalderson@freeuk.com www.swaledale-sheep.com

Teeswater Sheep Breeders' Association

Mrs. M. S. Braithwaite *(Secretary)*, Wodencroft,
Cotherstone, Barnard Castle, Co. Durham, DL12 9UQ
Tel: 01833 650032 wodencroft@freenet.co.uk
www.teeswater-sheep.co.uk

Badger Face Welsh Mountain Sheep Society

Miss Lucy Levinge *(Secretary)*, Stall House, Vowchurch,
Herefordshire, HR2 0QD Tel: 01981 550685
lucy-levinge@fwi.co.uk www.badgerfacesheep.co.uk
gpjcilhir@aol.com (Gwyn Jones - publicity officer)

Showing Sheep

Wensleydale Sheep Society
Coffin Walk, Sheep Dip Lane, Princethorpe,
Warwickshire, CV23 9SP Tel: 01926 633439
www.wensleydale-sheep.com

Whiteface Dartmoor Sheep Breeders' Association
Gordon Chambers *(Secretary)*
www.whitefacedartmoorsheep.co.uk

Shows Staging Sheep Classes

There are dozens of shows taking place throughout
the summer that stage classes for sheep. Some of the
major ones are listed below. Only the month has been
included as the date varies a little each year. All details
were correct at the time of writing.

You can also find a more complete listing, including
dates, at the Association of Show and Agricultural
Organisations' excellent website - www.asao.co.uk

May

Leicestershire County Show
The Show Office, Dishley Grange, Derby Road,
Loughborough, Leics., LE11 5SF Tel: 01509 646 786
info@leicestershireshow.co.uk
www.leicestershireshow.co.uk

South Suffolk Agricultural Show
Mr. G. Bailes, 35 Dalham Road, Moulton, Suffolk, CB8 8SB
Tel: 01638 750879 www.southsuffolkshow.co.uk

Devon County Show
Mrs. O. Allen Tel: 01392 446000
info@westpoint-devonshow.co.uk
www.devoncountyshow.co.uk

Hertfordshire County Show
The Hertfordshire Agricultural Society, The Showground,
Dunstable Road, Redbourn, Herts., AL3 7PT
Tel: 01582 792626 office@hertshow.com
www.hertsshow.com

Northumberland County Show
Mrs. G. Shotton, Hexham Auction Mart, Tynegreen,
Hexham, Northumberland, NE46 3SG Tel: 01434 604216
info@northcountyshow.co.uk
www.northcountyshow.co.uk

Surrey County Show
Mrs. S. Ashworth, 8 Birtley Courtyard, Bramley,
Guildford, Surrey, GU5 0LA Tel: 01483 890810
scas@surreycountyshow.co.uk
www.surreycountyshow.co.uk

Royal Cornwall Show
Mr. C. P. Riddle, The Royal Cornwall Showground,
Wadebridge, Cornwall, PL27 7JE Tel: 01208 812183
info@royalcornwall.co.uk
www.royalcornwall.co.uk

Showing Sheep

June

Three Counties' Show
The Three Counties' Agricultural Society, The Showground, Malvern, Worcs., WR13 6NW Tel: 01684 584900 info@threecounties.co.uk, www.threecounties.co.uk

Cheshire County Show
Mr. N. Evans, Clay House Farm, Flittogate Lane, Tabley, Knutsford, Cheshire, WA16 0HJ Tel: 01565 650200 info@cheshirecountyshow.org.uk www.cheshirecountyshow.org.uk

Royal Highland Show
Royal Highland Centre, Ingliston, Edinburgh, EH28 8NB Tel: 0131 335 6200 www.royalhighlandshow.org

Royal Norfolk Show
Norfolk Showground, Dereham Road, Norwich, NR5 0TT Tel: 01603 748931 www.royalnorfolkshow.co.uk

July

The Royal Show
The Royal Agricultural Society of England, Stoneleigh Park, Warks., CV8 2LZ Tel: 02476 858282 www.royalshow.org.uk

The Great Yorkshire
The Great Yorkshire Showground, Wetherby Rd., Harrogate, North Yorkshire Tel: 01423 541000, info@yas.co.uk www.greatyorkshireshow.co.uk

Kent County Show
Kent Showground, Maidstone, Kent, ME14 3JF
Tel: 01622 630975 info@kentshowground.co.uk,
www.kentshowground.co.uk

Ashby-de-la-Zouch & District Agricultural Society
Mrs. L. A. Ensor, Tithe Farm Livery Stables, Ashby Road,
Boundary, Swadlincote, Derbyhire Tel: 01283 229225
info@ashbyshow.com www.ashbyshow.com

Newport Show
Mrs. C. Farrell, Newport and District Agricultural Society,
2 Market Mews, Newport, Shropshire, TF10 7EY
info@newportshow.co.uk www.newportshow.co.uk

Royal Welsh Show
The Royal Welsh Agricultural Society, Llanelwedd,
Builth Wells, Powys, LD2 3SY Tel: 01982 553683
info@rwas.co.uk www.rwas.co.uk

New Forest & Hampshire County Show
The Showground, New Park, Brockenhurst, Hampshire,
SO42 7QH Tel: 01590 622400 info@newforestshow.co.uk
www.newforestshow.co.uk

August

North Devon Show
Mrs. D. Siggs, Secretary, PO Box 295, Barnstaple, Devon,
EX3 2BS Tel: 01769 560205 www.northdevonshow.com

Bakewell Show
The Showground, Bakewell, Derbyshire, DE45 1AQ
Tel: 01629 812736/7 info@bakewellshow.org
www.bakewellshow.org

Showing Sheep

Anglesey County Show

Anglesey Agricultural Showground, Ty Glyn Williams, Gwalchmai, Anglesey, LL65 4RW Tel: 01407 720072 info@angleseyshow.org.uk www.angleseyshow.org.uk

Pembrokeshire County Show

County Showground, Withybush, Haverfordwest, SA62 4BW Tel: 01437 764331 www.pembrokeshirecountyshow.co.uk

Epworth & District Agricultural Show

Mr. D. A. Poulter, 38 High Street, Belton, Doncaster, DN9 1LR Tel: 01427 872571 www.epworthshow.org

Melplash Agricultural Show

Mrs. A. Ford Tel: 01308 423337 secretary@melplashshow.co.uk www.melplashow.co.uk

September

Wolsingham & Wear Valley Agricultural

Mr. H. G. Dobson, 37 Lydgate Lane, Wolsingham, Bishop Auckland, Co. Durham, DL13 3LF Tel: 01388 527862 www.wolsinghamshow.com

Dorset County Show

Agriculture House, Acland Road, Dorchester, DT1 1EF Tel: 01305 264249 secretary@dorsetcountyshow.co.uk www.dorsetcountyshow.co.uk

Llandysul & District Agricultural Show

Miss B. Davies, Tynewydel, Gorrig, Llandysul, SA44 4JP Tel: 07901716957 www.llandysulshow.co.uk

Westmorland County Show
Westmorland County Agricultural Society, Lane Farm,
Crooklands, Milnthorpe, Cumbria, LA7 7HN
Tel: 01539 567804 www.westmorland.co.uk

Royal County of Berkshire Show
Newbury Showground, Priors Court, Hermitage,
Thatcham, Berks., RG18 9QZ Tel: 01635 247111
office@newburyshowground.co.uk
www.newburyshowground.co.uk

Stokesley Agricultural Show
Mrs. J. Hugill, 38 West Green, Stokesley, Middlesbrough,
Cleveland, TS9 5BD Tel: 01642 713209
www.stokesleyshow.co.uk

Showing Sheep

Rare Breed Shows and Sales

These are held in September and October. The main ones are:

Carlisle Rare Breed Sale
Harrison & Hetherington, Borderway Mart, Rosehill, Carlisle, CA1 2RS Tel: 01228 640924 info@borderway.com
www.livestock-sales.co.uk

Melton Mowbray Traditional & Native Breeds
Melton Mowbray Market, Scalford Road, Melton Mowbray, LE13 1JY Tel: 01664 562971
 sales@meltonmowbraymarket.co.uk
www.meltonmowbraymarket.co.uk

Chelford Rare & Traditional Breeds
Agricultural Centre, Chelford, Cheshire Tel: 01625 861122
Fax: 01625 860079 chelford@frankmarshall.co.uk
www.frankmarshall.co.uk

York Rare & Minority Breeds
York Auction Centre, Murton, York, YO19 5GF
Tel: 01904 489731 rarebreeds@stephenson.co.uk
www.ylc.co.uk

The Good Life Pres Ltd.
P O Box 536
Preston
PR2 9ZY
01772 652693

The Good Life Press publishes a wide range of titles for the smallholder, farmer and country dweller as well as Home Farmer, the monthly magazine for anyone who wants to grab a slice of the good life - whether they live in the country or the city.

Other titles that may be of interest

A Guide to Traditional Pig Keeping by Carol Harris
An Introduction to Keeping Cattle by Peter King
An Introduction to Keeping Sheep by J Upton/D Soden
Build It! by Joe Jacobs
Craft Cider Making by Andrew Lea
First Buy a Field by Rosamund Young
Flowerpot Farming by Jayne Neville
Grow and Cook by Brian Tucker
How to Butcher Livestock and Game by Paul Peacock
Making Jams and Preserves by Diana Sutton
Precycle! by Paul Peacock
Talking Sheepdogs by Derek Scrimgeour
The Bread and Butter Book by Diana Sutton
The Cheese Making Book By Paul Peacock
The Pocket Guide to Wild Food by Paul Peacock
The Polytunnel Companion by Jayne Neville
The Sausage Book by Paul Peacock
The Shepherd's Pup (DVD) with Derek Scrimgeour
The Smoking and Curing Book by Paul Peacock
The Urban Farmer's Handbook by Paul Peacock
A Cut Above the Rest (Butchering DVD)

www.goodlifepress.co.uk
www.homefarmer.co.uk

An Introduction to Keeping Sheep

By Jayne Upton and Denis Soden

Contents

ISBN 978 1 904871 22 4